"Rob Wildwood has a burning passion for
those connected to the Fae realms. His fearless explorations of wild and often remote locations enable others to experience these places through his stunning recollections and photographic images."

~ Karen Kay, author, 'Oracle of the Fairies' (Hay House 2019), editor of Fae Magazine and organiser of 3 Wishes Faery Festival in Cornwall

"Feel your mystic-self stir from deep within as 'The Land of the Fae' beckons you through its pages into an ancient and mystical world. Glimmers of ancient memories surface as Rob Wildwood reveals the hidden doorways and secret places that are found betwixt and between the worlds, as he shares with us his personal and fascinating explorations of the mystical and very magical British Isles.

Packed with secret tips of where to find Fairies, how to acknowledge and commune with them, this honest and magical guide is the book that fairy seekers everywhere have been waiting for!

The faeries are waiting in the waterfalls, the streams, in every meadow, garden and forest. They wait for you in the caves and hills, skies and oceans. They are present in every flower, each leaf, blade of grass and every rock and stone. Will you not acknowledge them and take a step sideways to become part of their magic? Time to take this handy book and go explore, investigate and pursue adventure as a new glittering path is revealed..."

~ Flavia Kate Peters, author, 'Connecting with the Fairies Made Easy: Discover the Magical World of the Nature Spirits' (Hay House 2018), 'Way of the Faery Shaman' (Moon Books 2015), 'Faery Godmother oracle deck' (Solarus/Llewelyn 2017)

'The Land of the Fae is a wonderful and truly visionary adventure exploring the magical landscape of the British Isles and its Otherworldly kin. This initiatory tale of Rob's marvelous first hand experiences is filled to the brim with Faery enchantment. A delightful read!'

Danu Forest, traditional Celtic Wisewoman, teacher and author of Gwyn ap Nudd, Wild God of Faery, (Moon Books) and Celtic Tree Magic (Llewellyn Worldwide).

The Land of the Fae

Merlin's Quest

Rob Wildwood

WYLDWOOD PUBLISHING

Glastonbury, UK

Published in 2019 by
Wyldwood Publishing
Glastonbury, UK

Rob Wildwood's pages:
themagicalplaces.com
https://www.facebook.com/themagicalplaces

ISBN : 978-0-9575433-1-7 (Paperback Edition)

Written and experienced by Rob Wildwood
Editing and design by Rob Wildwood
Transcribing by Jennifer Hunter
Formatting by Salah-Eddin Gherbi
Cover artwork by Angie Latham - www.celticmystery.co.uk
Artwork for Wheel of the Year and Classification of Fae by Yannick Dubois - www.yannickdubois.com

Also by Rob Wildwood

Magical Places of Britain (2013) - Wyldwood Publishing

The companion guide to the Land of the Fae! A beautifully illustrated photographic guide to some of Britain's most magical places including many of the places mentioned in this book.

Primal Awareness (2018) - Moon Books

A short history of mankind's separation from nature and what we can do to reconnect.

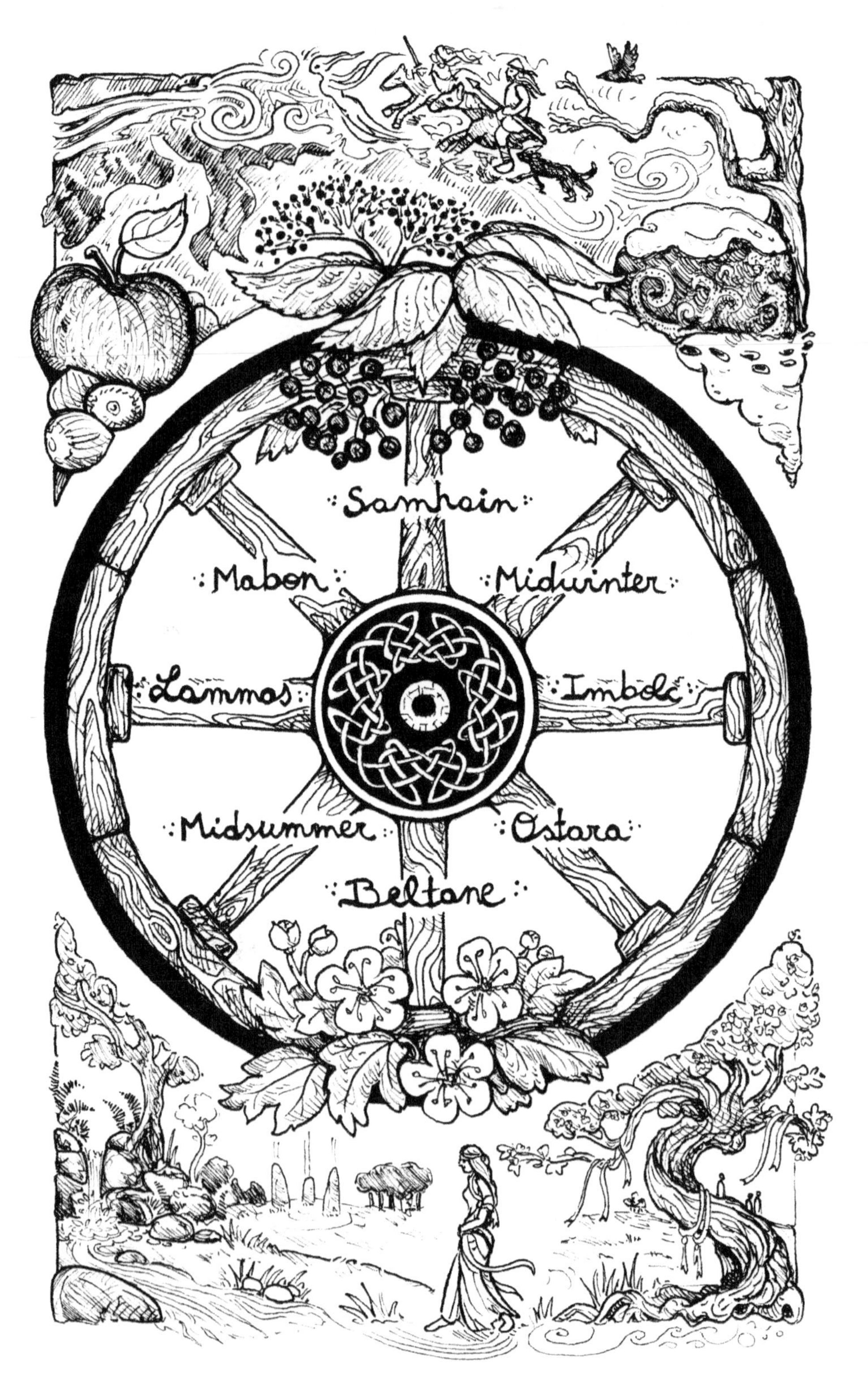

Samhain
Mabon
Midwinter
Lammas
Imbolc
Midsummer
Ostara
Beltane

Contents

Foreword

All of the events I am about to relate to you actually happened. Some of them occurred in our physical reality, while others occurred only in the world of spirit. These came to me as visions and direct experiences as I journeyed into the sacred landscape of Britain and tuned into the magical places that lie hidden within the landscape. The visions were revealed to me as the veil that separates our world from the Otherworld of the Fae was parted, allowing me to peer, for a brief moment, into their magical world.

To achieve these altered states I employed shamanic techniques including drumming and deep breathing, but there were no drugs involved, only a clearing of the mind, a deep state of meditation, and an openness to the spirits of each place.

At the start of my journey I had very little experience of this kind of work, but I decided from the outset that I would not question my experiences or over-analyse them, I would simply go with the flow and see where the journey took me.

Likewise the text has not been censored, I have related everything that happened to me at these sites, whether I felt it was relevant or not. Perhaps the reader will be able to unearth subtle messages which I have missed, or will be able to peer deeper into the mysteries of this land than I have been able to.

My visionary experiences in the Otherworld of the Fae I have printed in italics, while the rest of the text details my actual experiences in the physical world. Sometimes it was hard to tell what was real and what was not, so I hope that this will aid you as a guide.

So join me now as my journey begins...

Introduction

Let me take you on a journey to the Otherworld! A magical journey that will take us deep into the sacred landscape of Britain.

As we journey into this mysterious Otherworld we will encounter the magical beings that dwell there; the elves and the fairies, hobs and goblins, water nymphs and tree spirits.

Along the way we will be guided by the spirit of Merlin, and by faery queen Maeve. Animals and beings from the Otherworld will also illuminate our path as the true nature of our mission here on earth is slowly revealed to us. A mission that will uncover a whole Otherworld of magic and mystery hidden within the sacred landscape of Britain.

So join the journey and follow me now, into The Land of the Fae!

Merlin's Cave, Initiation into the Magic Circle

21st June - Summer Soltice

It was while sitting on the rocks by Merlin's cave in Tintagel Haven, Cornwall, waiting for the tide to go out, that I was initiated into Merlin's magic circle.

My new friends Alphedia and Auraengus were there, chatting away with some of the other folks who had followed us down to the shore. I had met them only a few days before, at 3 Wishes Faery Festival on Bodmin Moor where Alphedia had been giving a talk about the fairies and had been channelling the nature god Pan. They had come here to Tintagel to perform a ritual in Merlin's cave, but right now the tide was in, and so the cave was made inaccessible by the waves.

As I listened to the crashing of the waves on the shore I closed my eyes and felt myself being transported to an Otherworldly realm...

I could see myself walking through a dark forest of twisted trees and gnarled roots that seemed to go on forever; but soon I saw a golden light ahead that seemed to be coming from a huge clearing like an arena. I stepped forward into the forest clearing and could see a golden yellow band of light ahead of me, encircling the entire arena like a shimmering golden ring. I stepped into the band of golden light and saw my world turn yellow and hazy before my eyes, and as I stepped out of the other side I was greeted by the most astonishing sight that I had ever seen!

A huge baying crowd of the most fantastical magical creatures were gathered there in a mighty host, forming a deep crowd around a clear central area as if awaiting the start of some great performance. All the demons in hell and all the mythical beings of faerie could not have rivalled this crowd. I saw goats' heads, dragon wings and tiger bodies; horns, hooves, fangs and feelers; creatures tall and spindly like giant birds, or small and red-faced like angry leprechauns. Tooth, claw, colour and chaos. It was more than I could possibly take in, but as I drew nearer and stepped through the crowd my eyes alighted upon a lone figure standing in the centre of the field.

He was dressed in deep blue robes and a skull cap, and kept raising his arms to the cloudy skies as if performing some heathen ritual. I knew in my heart that this was the wizard Merlin. As I broke through to the front of the crowd I noticed he was carrying a wand in his left hand which he suddenly pointed in my direction. He turned to face me and gently beckoned me forward.

Hesitantly I stepped into the arena. The crowd were roaring now, shaking their fists, stamping up and down, and flapping their grotesque wings. Merlin stood there with his arms outstretched and greeted me like an old friend. I knelt before him and he asked me if I accepted this initiation into his magic circle.

A hundred thoughts tried to enter my head all at the same time, doubts, fears and more, but I knew why I was here, my path was clear. I simply shut all the thoughts out and said, "I do."

I had no idea what path lay ahead of me, I just knew that it was one which my soul was called to follow, and I was open to experiencing whatever came my way, for good or ill.

As I spoke my affirmation he tapped me on the head three times with his wand and the crowd gave a huge cheer. As simple as it was, my initiation was now complete.

This was to be the start of a magical journey that would lead me to many of the most wild, remote and fantastical places in the British Isles and beyond. A mission that would only be revealed to me slowly, and which would at times seem senseless and without direction, while at other times would make me feel like the very mysteries of the universe were being revealed to me.

I opened my eyes and found myself back on the shoreline in Tintagel. Alphedia had facilitated my initiation with Merlin by tapping me on the forehead with her crystal wand and sending me off into a deep trance.

After this Otherwordly experience, I stripped off and went for a dip in the cold seawater by the cave entrance. My new friends thought I was a bit crazy, but I was enjoying the icy bite of the water on my skin. I disappeared behind a large boulder but the lapping waves were now coming up to my head so I decided to turn back for the shore to dry off and warm up in the sun.

Over tea and cakes in the beach-side café we shared some stories before heading back to our accommodation to freshen up and await the evening's low tide.

* * *

We returned later in the day and the tide was now far out. The sandy cave entrance looked invitingly mysterious. The cave was broad and tall, about 20-30ft high, and it passed right under the headland that carried Tintagel Castle high above, the supposed birthplace of King Arthur. The cave continued all the way out to the other side of the headland where daylight could just be seen filtering through and the crashing of the waves on the far side could faintly be heard.

We entered, and the sandy entrance soon gave way to an uneven rocky surface containing several large rock-pools.

As I gazed around, exploring the cave's hidden wonders, Alphedia stepped up to one of the rock-pools, and after a while, eyes closed and arms by her sides, started to sing a gentle and enchanting tune of a kind that I'd never heard before. It was as if, in a trance, the fairies were singing through her and enchanting the whole cave. I left Alphedia and Auraengus behind and travelled as far as I could through the cave until the rocks became too jagged and slippery for me to safely continue, but I could see the ocean ahead on the far side of the cave. I was quite new to all this spiritual stuff and still fairly embarrassed by it, so I chose to find my own quiet corner of the cave in which to meditate. Standing there I closed my eyes and altered my breathing, and was soon carried away by the melodious sound of Alphedia's enchanted singing, distantly echoing from the far end of the cave.

Suddenly the water ahead of me erupted and I saw the sea god Neptune rise up out of the waves! Bare-chested, bearded and wearing a golden crown he smelled of seaweed and the ocean's depths. The water cascaded from his trident and torso as he rose up to fill the entire entrance of the cave, like a mighty god of old.

"Fetch me my undines!" he bellowed, his voice booming and echoing around the whole chamber.

In my vision, I could see his mermaid helpers, fishy-tailed and seaweed haired, swimming towards him under the waves. Not beautiful maidens like they are in fairy tales, but half fish, half human creatures of the salty depths.

Then as soon as he had appeared he was gone, crashing back down under the waves the same way that he had arisen.

"What was the significance of this?" I wondered. Why had the god of the sea presented himself to me and commanded me like that? I guessed that would have to remain a mystery for now.

Alphedia stopped singing, but she was still standing by the pool with her eyes closed, deep in meditation. After a while she opened her eyes and I had to ask her where she had learnt such beautiful music.

"The fairies taught it to me!" she replied.

How could I deny it?

Alphedia closed her eyes again while Auraengus busied himself in the sandy entrance, carving strange sigils into the sand.

Wondering what to do I sat down on a rock and closed my eyes again.

Almost instantly another titanic figure rose up out of the pool ahead of me, filling the cave so that he had to crook his neck up against the ceiling! From the goat's legs and horned head that peered down at me from the roof of the cave I instantly recognised him as the god Pan, lord of nature. His great smelly goat's legs seemed to fill the cave, his huge cloven feet planted firmly on the rocks before me. He didn't speak, he just looked down at me, smiling.

"Could this day get any stranger?" I thought. Alphedia had finished her meditation now and was about to start the ritual that Auraengus had been preparing. Alphedia told me that three witches had been trapped in this cave long ago, their spirits forced to reside here all these long ages, but now it was time for them to be moved on into the light. We would be performing a ritual to facilitate this, and we would be doing it now in the magic hexagram (six pointed star) that Auraengus had laid out in the sand.

We each performed our part in the ritual as instructed, and when it was over Alphedia told me that it had been a success, the witches had been successfully moved on, and our good deed was done for the day!

The spirit of Merlin then visited each of us in turn, and presented each of us with a magical crystal that would aid us in our quest.

By now the sun was going down and the day was drawing to a close, and what an extraordinary day it had turned out to be! I had never done anything like this before, but somehow it all seemed natural, I just accepted it and went along with it, wondering what would happen next!

I knew one thing though, after this day my life would never be the same again.

Dundon Beacon, Encounter with a Tree Spirit

24th July

I travelled back through Cornwall and Devon and then decided to spend some time in Glastonbury, Somerset. Glastonbury had become a home from home for me, with its magical Tor and healing wells, but now I was feeling drawn to an enchanting little village nearby called Compton Dundon. Its churchyard contains a huge and ancient yew tree and there is a magical wooded hill there known as Dundon Beacon which was calling to me.

I climbed up through the magical forest of oak, hazel and ash which lines the flanks of Dundon Beacon and eventually came to a clearing dominated by two huge horse-chestnut trees.

By the side of the clearing water issued forth from a little spring forming a small patch of fresh clear water that ran away in a rivulet. It seemed like the ideal place to try out my new-found abilities, and so I made an offering to the spring and then sat down and meditated with the crystal that had been given to me by Merlin.

I sensed the forest all around me, its aliveness and vitality, and in the tree in front of me I sensed the presence of a powerful tree spirit.

I felt slightly disappointed that the only thing I picked up on was the presence of a tree spirit in the large horse-chestnut nearest to me. I was in a forest so nothing unusual there I thought! However I decided to go over to the tree and investigate it more closely. What a shock I got when carved into the opposite side of the tree was a huge face looking just like a pagan god of old! This was surely a sacred grove of some kind.

I made offerings to the tree spirit, placed crystals around it to make a portal and then meditated while holding my hands against it.

Immediately I felt my spirit enter the tree and become one with it. My form took on the size and shape of the tree and I was looking down upon the clearing from high in the canopy. Beneath me in the clearing I could see little glowing forms scurrying around the place going about their daily tasks. They were the gnomes and other elementals that inhabited this place.

I felt like I was peering directly into the Otherworld, the world normally only visible to those with second sight, and was watching the elementals and other nature spirits going about their business. What a gift to experience such a thing in this magical place!

On my way home I asked for permission to cut myself a wand of hazel wood. My request was granted by the tree and so I took a small length of wood. Later on I fashioned it into a hazel wand with a pointed end and runes carved into it. I knew then that this would become a valuable and powerful tool in my spiritual work.

Black Hope Glen, The Horned God

28th July

Alphedia had invited me to come up and visit her. She lived with her husband Auraengus in the Scottish Borders, not far from Edinburgh.

Once I had crossed the border into Scotland I decided to visit a spectacular waterfall known as the Grey Mare's Tail, but during my little detour I was drawn to a mysterious looking valley called Black Hope Glen.

I drove up the isolated, windswept Scottish glen in my 4x4 vehicle (a Toyota Hilux with roof tent which I used for all of my adventures) and then stopped near the head of the glen and climbed up a remote gully that contained a few hidden trees and a tumbling rivulet of fresh, clear mountain water.

Eventually I came to a hidden pool that was completely isolated from the outside world. There I made an offering into the pool and then sat down and meditated.

A green man with stag horns appeared by the pool sitting cross-legged. He told me that he was the spirit of the land, of Albion, and of all living things here, but that his power had been fragmented by the building of roads and other obstacles. What had once been an all powerful spirit of the land had now been reduced to a mere shadow of his former self.

Perhaps he wanted me to do something about this? But what could I do? I couldn't get a direct answer, so I knew that this was something I would have to work out for myself.

I walked back down to my car and drove out of the valley, but not before being confronted by the local landowner on his quad bike, who asked me what I had been up to. What could I say? That I had been connecting with the spirit of the land and had been given a mission to help protect and restore the earth? Somehow I don't think he would have understood so I simply assured him that I had not been poaching, and moved on.

Findhorn and the Ancient Caledonian Pine Forests

3th August

While driving up to Findhorn in the North of Scotland to attend a course to learn more about nature spirits I took a detour through the ancient Abernethy pine forest.

The ancient woodland was mysterious and enchanting, with huge gnarly trees and open spaces between them where animals could wander. The forest was nothing like the impenetrable mono-culture plantations that we are nowadays more familiar with. But unfortunately the forest was dying; overgrazing by sheep and deer meant that almost no new trees were now growing. Eventually the existing pines will die of old age and there will be no more ancient pine forest remaining. Short of fencing off the whole forest, only drastic culling of the wild deer or the reintroduction of natural predators such as wolves could start to reverse the decline.

Luckily I found a gate that had been left open and so I entered the woodland in my 4x4 vehicle and drove through it on rough forest tracks until I came out the other side, high up on the wild Ryvoan Pass overlooking Glen More.

Ancient pine trees still clung to the hillsides there up in this wild and remote place. I was drawn to one particularly ancient specimen, sitting there like a sentinel overlooking the pass, and I tuned in to its energy.

I was told that the pine trees were retreating but they were not yet defeated. Some healing and some energy would help to facilitate regrowth and resurgence, and the eventual recolonisation of the land by wild nature.

So I laid my hands against the tree and sent healing white light into it and into the whole forest, setting my intention that it should grow and thrive once more.

I arrived later that evening in Findhorn and during my visit I learned more about connecting with nature spirits and elementals. On Saturday we tuned in to the nature spirits in the gardens and got messages from Pan, the horned god of nature, and then on Sunday we went to the beach to meet the mermaids, spirits of the ocean. Amazingly some seals were already there waiting for us, heads bobbing out of the water as they inspected us. To me this was confirmation that we were being greeted by the ocean spirits! I felt drawn to wade out into the deep icy-cold water to connect with them and to commune with the ocean spirits and as I returned to shore I noticed a shiny white pebble washed up on the sand. I was told, to keep it, and so I named it my 'selkie stone' after the seal maidens that delivered it to me.

* * *

On the way back from Findhorn I decided to visit another ancient pine forest, this time in Glen Affric.

I camped alone far up in the glen and was awoken in the dead of night by a strange whorling sound like nothing I had ever heard before, and it was coming from right outside my tent!

"WhooWhooWHOOwoowoowoowoowoowoo!"
"WhooWhooWHOOwoowoowoowoowoowoo!"

An eerie noise like that made by a bullroarer or sound hose.

I poked my head out of the tent but could see nothing. The sound seemed to be coming from near and far at the same time. I climbed out and followed the sound into the trees where I was sure it was coming from, but I didn't seem to be getting any closer. I ended up following the sound in all directions for a couple of hundred yards but found nothing.

Sometimes it sounded like some strange being was flying right around my head! Strange indeed! But I could not explain it...

The next day I explored more of Glen Affric, before travelling on to Plodda falls. There was an overhanging platform there that enabled me to stand right over the gushing waterfall as it plunged down into a deep gorge!

I then climbed to the bottom of the falls and gazed up into the cascading stream of water.

I felt myself enter the top of the waterfall and started dancing with all the tiny water sprites that drew their energy from rushing and cascading water. Behind the waterfall there seemed to be a passage leading into the realm of Faerie. I started to enter but didn't feel confident enough to travel far. What if I couldn't find my way back and became trapped there?

I would leave the experience of entering the Otherworld for another day...

Lindsaylands Hill, Fairy Releasement

7th August

I returned to Alphedia's house in the Scottish Borders and later in the afternoon I took her little black dog Romany out for a walk in the grassy hills nearby. I soon found the ruins of some old stone-built houses that were located beneath a hill capped with a few sparse trees and rocky outcrops. I climbed up to the summit and beneath the roots of one of the trees I found a large rabbit hole. The hole looked quite magical and inviting so I decided to try to journey into the Otherworld using some of the shamanic techniques I had recently learnt. The result was nothing like I expected though...

I had trouble entering the hole as it seemed to be blocking me somehow. So I mentally removed the blockage and instantly out of the hole shot hundreds of fairies, shining air elementals glowing with a bright white light! They shot up into the sky in a seemingly endless stream, as if being blown aloft on huge column of rushing air. Finally the gushing stream of glowing fairies came to an end and they all drifted high up in the sky like seeds blown from a dandelion clock, spreading as far as the eye could see in all directions. Slowly they drifted back down to Earth settling like cherry blossoms all over the land, reinvigorating it and bringing it back to life.

It was a truly magical experience but it seemed like I would need further help before I could successfully journey into the Otherworld, and so I asked Alphedia to guide me.

Glourourem Wood, Faery Wizards

8th August

The next day I told Alphedia about my attempts to enter the Otherworld, and the fears that could be holding me back. So she told me she would take me to her local woods where she knew there was an entrance to the Land of Faerie

We drove to Biggar Common, parked near Glourourem Wood and then walked over to where two trees formed a magic gateway. We left an offering of chocolate there, (but apparently they would have preferred cheese!) and were then given permission to step through...

A faery gatekeeper met us there and escorted us through the liminal zone that separates our world from the Otherworld of the Fae. Alphedia told me that it was important that we remembered which way we came through as we did not want to get lost in Faeryland! Alphedia said that we were being taken to a part of the wood that she hadn't been to before. We came to another gateway and after waiting to get permission we stepped through into the Otherworld.

We were met there by three faery wizards. These were the tall, human-sized faeries known as the Sidhe or Seelie Court Faeries. They asked us for our help and said they wanted us to work for them. Without hesitation we agreed and then we both had faerie wands implanted in our hearts. They told us that we would now become more sensitive to the pollution in the environment and chemicals in our food etc. They told us that the time was coming when their power would return, when nature wild and unpolluted would once more cover the land, and that we were to aid them in this.

We then carefully made our way back out of the woods, making sure that we took exactly the same route out that we had entered by.

Combe Hollow, Badgers and Wasps

19th August

I returned to Glastonbury and went for a walk one evening down Combe Hollow, in the woods near Compton Dundon. There I found some badger sets covered in old vines, with many trackways used by the badgers radiating out in all directions.

I walked around the woods until dusk and then was drawn to an old tree stump down a steep slope in the bottom of the hollow. I scrambled down to inspect it and then sat on top of it meditating. What had drawn me here I wondered? I walked around the tree stump several times until I noticed a hole at the base of it, I peered inside the hole and deep inside, at about arm's length was wedged a plastic bottle! How did that get in there? I reached inside and tried to pull the bottle out but it was firmly wedged in, I wriggled it around and pulled harder and finally it came out. It was clear that it had been there for a long time.

"So what was the point of that?" I thought. I sat there looking at the tree stump and wondered... and then as I sat looking small wood wasps started to fly from the hole which I had just made. First one or two, and then dozens of them! I was startled at first, thinking that they meant to sting me but I soon realised that they meant me no harm! It's strange but there were definitely no wasps here when I had first inspected the tree stump. Had I released them? I certainly sensed that they felt happy to be freed. It reminded me of the fairies I had released while up in Scotland. Was that a premonition of this event? What strange compulsion had led to me this remote tree stump to free these wasps, and what significance did it have?

As I walked back in the near darkness, pondering these thoughts, I heard some snuffling in the undergrowth. I stood stock still and after a while a badger appeared on the bank right opposite me. We stood staring at each other for a while and then exchanged greetings. "Thank you," he told me. I felt like I worked for the Fae now and for all of nature. I was doing their work, I was one of them.

St. Ninnian's Cave

28th August

St. Ninian, is an early Celtic saint who preached to the Picts in the 5th century. On the south west coast of Scotland, in Dumfries and Galloway, there is a shallow sea cave which is dedicated to him. I had first heard about St. Ninnian's cave from a druid called Damh the Bard at a pagan event known as the Artemis Gathering. "It is said you can hear the voice of God in there," he told us, "and it's true!" Intrigued I decided to pay a visit, so on my next trip to Scotland I took a detour into Dumfries and Galloway.

Unfortunately I arrived there at the most inconvenient time. Once a year the local bishop holds a service in the cave and as I arrived they were just setting up the marquee and stage! Undaunted I passed them by and wandered into the shallow sea cave. Once inside I had a look at some of the old rock carvings and Christian offerings that had been left there, including some crude crucifixes made from a pair of twigs. After a while the people setting up the stage wandered off, so I had the place to myself at last.

As I lay down in the back of the cave the hooded form of a monk entered. It was St. Ninnian! He had come here to explain to me the true meaning of 'Christ consciousness'. He said that attaining Christ consciousness is the realisation that we are all spiritual beings and that matter, as we perceive it, is not reality. He told me that the Christian cross is a symbol of this, it represents the death of the physical body and awaking to the realisation of Christ consciousness. The crucifixion of Christ was simply an allegory showing that Christ rejected his physical body and embraced totally the spiritual. The early Celtic church was aware of this, and did not take the bible as literally as people did later on.

It was quite a revelation to me and made me look at Christianity in a whole new light. People have a terrible habit of taking allegorical tales literally and this has caused so much strife and conflict over the centuries. Once we understand spirituality and realise that the material world of our five senses is just an illusion, then we can dispense with religious texts and instead become aware of the deeper spiritual meanings behind them.

My path was a pagan one but St. Ninian reminded me that I should remain open to the wisdom of all spiritual teachings and not simply reject them.

Cup and Ring Marked Stone

29th August

While I was up in Dumfries and Galloway I decided to visit one of the local cup & ring marked stones that was carved by the ancient ancestors of the Picts.

As I sat by the stone I had a vision of Neolithic people grinding the grooves by hand using a rounded rock, and as they did so they were putting energy into the land at a point somewhere in the distance. Once they had carved the central cup then they amplified its power by carving the ring marks around it. New cup marks had to be created each time they performed this ceremony, which explained why there were so many of them covering so many rocks.

I later discovered that many dowsers hold the same belief, that cup-marked rocks somehow transfer energy from points of power to where it is needed. Dowsers have been able to follow these energy lines and find features on the landscape that correspond to the cup marks.

Merlindale

21st September - Autumn Equinox

Merlindale is a valley in the Scottish Borders that is associated with the story of Myrddin Wyllt, a Welsh name which is translated as Merlin the Wild or Merlin of the Woods. You may find it strange to have a Welsh name in the Scottish Borders but in fact the whole of lowland Scotland was once occupied by a Welsh speaking people, the Ancient Britons. However in this story he is not the powerful court wizard known from later Arthurian tales, but a half-crazed druid and prophet who lived like a wild man in the woods after suffering a terrible defeat in battle.

I came to Merlindale to attend a course that was run by Alphedia, where I hoped to learn more about this Merlin and make some kind of spiritual connection to him.

During one of the meditations, I had a vision of a white castle where I met with Merlin. He gave me a magical compass which he told me I should use to find the correct locations to bring down energy. This energy would be a kind of life force which would beam down to Earth from an extra-terrestrial source to animate the land and the life here.

I had no idea then how significant this was to become to my greater quest, but in time much more would be revealed to me.

Also, it was on this course, and on similar ones run by Alphedia, that I would meet the friends who would accompany me on some of my quests; Sara, Tina and others. After our meditations we climbed the nearby hill, on top of which stood the crumbled and blasted stone remains of Tinnis Castle. We performed a ceremony there and made small offerings of gold to the dragon at the top of the hill.

I could see the dragon sleeping beneath the hill, representing the powerful Earth energies there. Lines of power connected him to other similar sites.

I took out my hazel wood wand that I had hand-carved with runes and planted it on top of the hill.

Merlin immediately sent down a powerful column of white light, filling my wand with energy. The energy filled the entire hill, giving power to the dragon and to the dragon lines that connected this hill to other similar places.

* * *

The next day I returned alone to Tinnis Castle. Legend has it that the castle was blasted apart by gunpowder but I saw something quite different as I gazed into the past.

A column of white light, like an enormous lightning strike, crashing into the castle from above, blasting it apart...

The white light seemed to have something to do with the power and presence of Merlin, as if it were he that summoned down the lightning.

From the top of the castle I then surveyed the landscape laid out before me. I could see the River Tweed winding its way through the valley bottom and in front of it I could just make out a standing stone, known as Merlin's standing stone.

I climbed down from the hill and in the stone wall of the farm opposite I found a gap which, according to folklore, was made to allow free passage for the fairies as it lies on a fairy pathway. I wondered if the fairy pathway led to the standing stone, as it seemed to be heading in that direction? Could this be one of the energy lines that lead from Tinnis Castle?

I walked over to the standing stone and had a great view from there looking back to Tinnis Castle. Could this be lying on a ley line? I pondered the idea that this stone could be sitting on a one of the dragon lines, but at this stage I did not have the tools to confirm my suspicions.

I then visited a couple more sites in the area that were associated with Merlin of the Woods, including Merlin's grave by the river, and Merlin's altar stone, which sat hidden by the roadside and felt to me like it had once been used for animal sacrifice.

Merlin of the Woods was clearly a druid as in the original tale it is told that he dies the classic druidic triple death:

> "Myrddin Wyllt prophesied his own death, which would happen by falling, stabbing, and drowning. This was fulfilled when a gang of jeering shepherds drove him off a cliff, where he was impaled on a stake left by fishermen, and died with his head below water."

Schiehallion, The Faery Hill of the Caledonians

23rd September

There are many legends associated with this mysterious mountain in the centre of Scotland, but I came here to find a magical cave on its flank called Uamh Tom a'Mhor-fhir which has much local folklore attached to it concerning the fairies:

> "Of all the caves in the Parish, the most remarkable is that at Tom a Mhorair, on the south side of Glenmore, near the west shoulder of Schiehallion. It has a fairly wide opening which extends for three or four yards. It then contracts and slants into total darkness in the bowels of the earth. Some miles to the east of this there is another opening, which tradition holds to be the other end of the cave. According to the traditional accounts, this cave was regarded as an abode of fairies and other supernatural beings, rather than a hiding place of mortals. The only men who were supposed to have lived there were individuals who were believed to have been in league with supernatural powers."

> "Two hump-backed men lived on either side of the mountain, one near Braes of Foss and the other near Tempar. One fine summer's eve, the man from Braes of Foss went to visit his friend, walking through Gleann Mor. As he approached the cave - Uamh Tom a'Mhor-fhir - he heard the singing and dancing of fairies. He was totally thrilled and joined in the song in a melodious voice, adding a new line. The fairies were delighted with the addition and gave him three gifts - that he would be tall and lose his hump, that he would be healthy and that he would have plenty until he died."

> "There is a famous cave at the foot of Schiehallion where, tradition has it, fairies loved to dwell. There, it is said mortals from time to time dwelt among them, and interesting stories are told of the strange ways in which they were rescued from their power. Behind Schiehallion, again, on Creag Chionneachan, is one of the spots where the old Fingalian warriors were supposed to lie on their elbows awaiting the third blast of the horn that is

to raise them to life again"

"...Schiehallion (3,547 feet) - i.e. the hill of the Daoine Shi or the Fairies' Hill. If all the tales one hears related by old natives of Rannoch could be fully relied on, Schiehallion in days of yore used to be a favourite resort of the fairy folks, and more especially once a year, when all the various tribes throughout Glenlyon, Rannoch, Strathtummel, etc. congregated. Here they used to assemble in large numbers and hold their annual convocation, presided over by the beautiful and accomplished Queen Mab, gorgeously arrayed in her favourite green silk robes, with her abundant crop of beautiful golden-yellow hair waving in long ringlets over her shoulder down to her waist. It is said that there are a long series of mysterious caves, extending from one side of the mountain to the other."

"There is a very remarkable cave near the south-west angle of Sith-chaillinn [Schiehallion], at the 'Shealing,' called Tom-a-mhorair, or the Earl's eminence. Some miles to the east, there is an opening in the face of a rock, which is believed to be the termination thereof. Several stories are told and believed by the credulous, relating to this cave; that the inside thereof is full of chambers or separate apartments, and that, as soon as a person advances a few yards, he comes to a door, which, the moment he enters, closes, as it opened, of its own accord, and prevents his returning."

Well it doesn't get any more intriguing than that! So I set off into the mountains and managed to find a very rocky 4x4 track that led up from Fortinghall almost to the base of Schiehallion.

After driving for ten very bumpy kilometers I reached the end of the track and continued through the boggy ground on foot.

I then had to cross a small river to reach the old shielings where in times gone by the herders would have spent the summer with their sheep. I approached one of the shielings and performed a small ceremony, offering some food and crystals.

I could sense the presence of Queen Mab and she appeared there before me dressed in her green robes with long flowing golden hair. She told me I was to spread the word and publicise my faery knowledge, no longer should I keep it secret.

I have always remembered the words that Queen Mab spoke to me, but I was not really sure how to proceed at this stage. I was worried that publicising these sites could ruin them and take away their ancient magic.

I spent the rest of the afternoon looking for the cave, but no matter how hard I tried I could not find it! This really was a magical cave, perhaps it was hiding itself from me!

After speaking with the gamekeeper I returned the next day to try to find the cave again, and again it eluded me! I remembered the tales about how upon entering the cave the doors will close behind you and you won't be able to get out again, so maybe I was being protected from finding it! Or perhaps the fairies were just playing games with me?

I heard several accounts of people finding this cave, including the gamekeeper's own, but so far have not been able to find a single photo of it on the internet, despite its fame! Mysterious indeed! Maybe the time will be right for this cave to reveal itself one day, but it was not to be today!

Strathaven, Fairy Mound

3rd October

Directly south of the village of Strathaven, in a hidden bend of the Avon Water, lies a fairy mound that local people still venerate.

I travelled there with Alphedia, Aurengus and their dog Romany, and after crossing several fields and a few barbed-wire fences we arrived at the mound, a natural outcrop of rock jutting from a green meadow by the river

We were surprised to meet a local family there who, following an old tradition, were walking three times sunwise around the mound to show their respect to the fairies. We did the same and also planted some crystals around the mound.

Alphedia and I climbed to the top only to discover that careless people had started a fire up there and burnt all the bushes while leaving broken bottles and litter lying all around. With the help of the local children we cleaned up all the litter and broken glass, and then sent healing to the place. Perhaps that is why we had been drawn here? I am sure the fairies were pleased with our work anyway, and we set a good example for the local children.

Romany had climbed up the side of the mound and was staring at a wall of rock. He had discovered a hidden entrance to the faery mound, but we felt that our work was done here for today and so we decided not to investigate further and left the faeries in peace.

It was heartwarming to find ancient traditions still surviving and being passed on to the children.

Hob Holes, Runswick Bay

8th October

A hob is a creature from the folklore of the north of England. He is a household spirit who is quite helpful to the land owners until they do something to annoy him, at which point he either leaves or starts to make their life a misery by bringing terrible misfortune. He is portrayed as being small and shaggy haired, wearing either very rough clothes or no clothes at all. He is similar to the Scottish brownie or the Swedish tomte.

In the cliffs of Runswick bay on the north coast of Yorkshire there are some small caves called Hob Holes. In times gone by local people would bring their children to Hob Holes to cure them from the whooping cough by reciting this rhyme:

> "Hob Hole Hob,
> My bairn's gotten t'kink cough,
> Tak it off,
> Tak it off."

I drove to the clifftop above Hob Holes and found an ancient trackway leading down to the beach. It was so overgrown with trees and bushes that it formed a kind of tunnel. It felt to me like some kind of ancient processional way.

I followed it down to the beach and then walked along the misty shoreline until I found the caves. I was drawn to one of the caves which seemed to go deeper than the others and despite its crumbling and precarious looking condition I decided to enter.

I crawled inside and then sat down at the end of the long damp tunnel, looking out at the shoreline.

I called out to the hob: "Hob Hole Hob! Hob Hole Hob!"

I had a vision of the hob coming to greet me. He looked like a mischievous little hobgoblin with long pointy ears, rather than one of the friendlier hobs I had read about in folklore! He was short and also had a long pointy nose and a droopy pointed cap. He eyed me suspiciously but he didn't have much to say, so I planted my wand into the sand in front of me and sent him healing energy. Because people no longer come here to ask the hob for healing it felt like he had lost his power and was slowly fading away. I felt like I was bringing him back to life again! He seemed to be happy that he was being acknowledged.

I felt like my work was done there so I crawled out of the tunnel and continued on down the beach. It was a mysterious and misty landscape of sand, seaweed and seabirds. I followed a steep gully inland into a totally wild landscape, the tiny watercourse led me deeper into the undergrowth until eventually I could go no further. The mist was clinging to spider's webs, covering them in dewy gemstones, as I surveyed this ancient landscape that was home to the mysterious hob.

St Fillan's Cave, Pittenweem

12th October

When I arrived back at Alphedia's place she had a message for me from spirit: "Visit St. Fillan's cave on Tuesday!" Neither of us knew where it was or indeed even what it was, so I looked it up on the internet and found out that there was a St. Fillan's cave in the small town of Pittenweem on the southern coast of Fife, Scotland.

So I made my way up there the following Tuesday and soon discovered the cave entrance beside a little street that ran down to the harbour.

The entrance was barred by a heavy iron gate emblazoned with a huge iron Celtic cross and it was inset with pieces of red hematite (iron ore)! My first impression was "Wow! Whatever is in there they REALLY don't want it getting out!" I remembered that the fairies are said to be repelled by iron, so I knew there was no way they would they be able to pass by this gate!

I wondered how I was going to get inside, but after asking some locals I soon discovered that the key was kept in the local cafe, which was also a chocolate shop. So I went to fetch the key, and then unlocked the gate and wandered into this strange cave.

Near the entrance was a painting and story about St. Fillan, while deeper inside was a natural sea cave that had been converted into a chapel with an altar.

In the past the cave had seen all kinds of uses, from a smugglers cave to a prison for witches, but it is most famous as the place where St. Fillan resided while he was converting the Picts. St Fillan could often be seen in the cave, so it was said, reading his parchments by the light of a strange glow that emanated from his hand!

I was disturbed a couple of times by tourists wandering in so eventually I decided to switch off the artificial lighting and lock the gate behind me. It certainly added to the spooky atmosphere!

With my torch (flashlight) in my hand I found another gate, which opened to a 'secret' passage out to another gate at the back. It led to an overgrown garden but again it was barred with iron and locked! So I returned to the chapel and left an offering on the altar, before crawling into the dark recesses at the back of the cave to meditate.

This cave is an entrance to the underworld. Spirits which were once able to roam in and out freely have now been imprisoned in here. I told these spirits not to be afraid and to follow me outside, but they were terrified of the iron gate. I literally had to lead them by the hand, one by one, past the gate, so that they could be free once more.

While in the back of the cave I noticed a small dripping spring of water which created a little flowstone pool which would make an excellent scrying mirror.

But I felt like my job was now done here, so left I left the cave and returned the key to the chocolate shop. Then a bizarre coincidence! Kalula, a woman I had met a couple of times at Alphedia's place was sitting in the chocolate shop drinking hot chocolate! What were the odds of meeting her in this cafe in this remote little town at this exact date and time? So I greeted her and told her about my experience in the cave. I was no longer getting shocked by these strange coincidences, which was just as well, for there were to be many more!

Dunino, pagan shrine and druid's den

13th October

I had heard about a famous pagan site in Fife called Dunino Den where once the druids had made their sacrifices. So while I was in the area I thought I would pay it a visit.

I parked my car by the main road and started walking through the woods. Right away I found a discarded candle lying on the path in front of me, which I picked up and took to be a positive sign. I followed the path through the woods, and along the edge of a gully until I came to an old church. I passed along the edge of the church and then walked down through the woods towards the deep gully.

The first thing I came to was a small circular pool that looked like an old stone well perched at the edge of the gully. I crouched down at the pool and meditated there. After a while I felt a great urge to thrust my hands into the cold water, and as I did so...

I suddenly felt like my hands had gripped the hilt of a great and majestic sword! I drew the sword from the water and was amazed to see it's shining blade and golden cross hilt studded with glittering gems! It was an etheric sword which I could use in the spirit world!

Months earlier I had sacrificed a real sword into a river as part of a ritual to break my ties with the past. Perhaps this spiritual weapon was what I was getting in return?

I left the pool and then walked down the so-called 'fairy steps' and into the druid's den itself. The place looked absolutely magical, a woodland glade hidden away by tall cliffs and bordered by a lively little burn (stream). The centre of the clearing was dominated by an upturned tree-stump inscribed with runes which was obviously being used as an altar.

All around the clearing people had left offerings of colourful beads, flags, ribbons etc. The rocks around the clearing had been adorned with Celtic crosses and other strange carvings, while every small crevice seemed to contain an offering of a coin or a shell.

At the base of one of the rock faces I found a tiny cave, only big enough to crawl inside on my belly.

Once inside, the cave opened up a little and I was able to twist around and look up into all the small crevices in the ceiling. They were filled with big shiny black spiders, black millipedes, midges and moths! I lit my candle in there, the one I had recently found, and settled down to meditate.

I started to see some small red-capped creatures, who tried to make contact with me.

But the midges (small biting flies) were bothering me so I batted them away with my hands... mistake! I don't think they liked that at all! I would have to learn to respect all the creatures of nature, no matter how small and bothersome. For all I knew they could have been fairies that I swatted!

As I lay back down I began to hear a deep rumbling sound that seemed to be coming from the earth. But the midges were relentless, and so, unable to focus, I decided to leave this claustrophobic place. I squeezed my way out and wandered back through the magical clearing. My meeting with the redcaps would have to wait for another day.

The Major Oak, Sherwood Forest

15th October

I arrived in Sherwood forest at dusk, just as the last of the tourists were leaving. In the darkening twilight I made my way along winding paths, past ancient oak trees until I arrived at the clearing containing the biggest oak tree of them all, the Major Oak.

This monster of a tree is so huge and ancient that it has to be propped up with wooden supports; it dominates the clearing and is surrounded by a low fence to keep tourists from damaging it.

There was no-one around at this time of the evening, so I slipped over the fence to take a closer look at this majestic old tree. As I walked around the tree I saw its huge limbs spread out above me, impossibly large and heavy, but still bearing fresh acorns despite its ancientness.

Then I noticed a huge fissure in the bark, I crept up to it and was able to squeeze inside and enter another world. The interior was huge. There was ample room to stand up straight or lie down flat. I noticed patches of fibreglass which presumably were placed there in an attempt to stop the rot and decay. I lay down on the floor, within the very bowels of the tree and tuned in...

I was approached by a pair of tiny redcaps, little humanoid figures, only eight and ten inches high. They looked like the pair that had tried to contact me at Dunino. They were squat creatures with impish faces and were dressed in simple peasant clothes. I asked them who they were but they just stared blankly at the ground in front of them. They seemed to me like a couple of tribesmen being questioned by someone from a totally alien culture whose language and motives they did not understand.

Suddenly one of them made a strange sound like an animal call: "Geee!"

Then the other smaller one, did the same: "Geee!"

Then both together rapidly one after the other: "Geee! Geee! Geee! Geee!"

I was perplexed and so I just said to them: "Take me to your world!" They still just stared at the ground, a look of non-comprehension on their faces, when suddenly one of them ran off, swiftly followed by the other. I followed them both and found myself on a broad path clinging to the edge of a mountainside. They ran off around a bend and as I followed them I just saw them disappear into a cave in the side of the mountain.

As I approached the cave I had a sense of foreboding. Something was in that cave and it wasn't pleasant! I could hear the redcaps in there still making their strange sounds: "Geee! Geee!" They seemed to be waiting for me to enter. I realised that I had no reason to trust these little creatures, and so I decided to return to the oak tree.

I really hadn't been expecting anything like this to happen and so I was unprepared when it did. It was a fascinating experience but I did not feel prepared to simply travel into the depths of the Underworld without a good reason. First I needed to discover my purpose here and why I was experiencing all these things.

Bardsey Island, Merlin's Cave

17th October

While researching more about Merlin on the internet I came across mention of a small cave on Bardsey Island (Ynnis Enli in Welsh) off the far tip of the Lynn peninsular in Wales. The cave was associated with Merlin who was said to be imprisoned on this island in his tower of glass, along with the thirteen treasures of Britain. I knew then that it was a place I had to visit! So the next day I set off on the long journey to north-west extremity of Wales...

Arriving at the very tip of the Lynn peninsular I was lucky enough to find a boatman to take me over the water to the island. The boatman, who had been brought up on the island, said he knew about the cave. He told me that the cave was very tiny and he had played in it as a child. He also told me a story about a local priest who had once lived in the cave as hermit, perhaps as a form of penance.

I asked the boatman if he had ever heard of any other strange occurrences on the island, but all he could tell me about were some lights which were often seen floating around from floor to floor of an old deserted cottage.

The boat rounded the island and pulled into a bay heavy with seaweed, we were then hauled up the slipway by a tractor and trailer.

The boatman pointed to the side of a nearby hill where I could just make out three white rocks forming a kind of triangle. The cave was there, just by those rocks, he told me.

I walked along the green lanes of this quiet, enchanting little island, past the occasional old whitewashed cottage until I came to a house called Plas Bach where a unique apple tree grows. The apples are unusually free from disease and grow nowhere else in the world apart from on this one tree. After asking around I found the tree, but unfortunately it did not bear any fruit at this time, so I took a small sprig of leaves to carry along with me for good luck. The tree is known by some as 'Merlin's Apple'.

Opposite the cottage, I followed a little passageway and started making my way up the heather-covered slope behind. By now I had lost sight of the triangle of white rocks and the hillside seemed to be criss-crossed with a maze of little trackways, so I was wondering how I was going to spot the place again.

As I climbed higher and higher I turned around and got a breathtaking view of the whole island, from the bay to my left where we had landed, to a far off rocky peninsular with its lighthouse, and all the way across to the haunted cottages and ruined abbey to my right.

Beneath me I could see black crow-like birds with long red curved beaks flying by, the famous choughs of Ynnis Enli. After more walking I came to three white rocks that seemed to match the ones I had seen earlier, so I started scanning around for a cave entrance. Beside one of the rocks I found a tiny little hole, barely big enough to sit up in.

I crawled inside, first on my hand and knees and then on my belly. It was pitch black inside so I was glad I was wearing my head torch.

After about three metres the passageway came to an end, so I scanned around with my torch to see what I could find. I explored all the hidden crevices and deep within one of them I found a crystal! A clear quartz point about two inches long and half an inch wide. Was this one of the thirteen treasures of Britain? Doubtful - it was likely just left there as an offering, but I preferred to think of it as a gift from Merlin and would very soon discover its usefulness...

To my left I found a ledge and above it a wide hole just big enough to crawl into. Brushing aside spiders' webs I managed to twist myself around and poke my head into the hole. I shone my torch down and discovered that the hole dropped down into a small chamber, just about big enough for two people to sit up in. As my torch shone down to the floor of the chamber I got a shock! There was the perfectly preserved skeleton of a sheep, lying exactly as it had died, but without a trace of flesh or wool on it. Instead there were just bare bones and a thin coating of green mould on the skull and spine. Judging by the state of the skeleton no-one had entered this chamber for a long, long time...

After my heart had stopped pounding I decided that I had to go in. Crawling in head first would have put me face to face with the mouldy sheep skull, so I decided upon entering feet first, with my back to the floor, head facing the ceiling. As my feet dropped down into the darkness I felt them crunch against the sheep skeleton and the spongy floor below... YUK... but I continued to ease myself in through the small gap until I got my whole body inside. I was now squatting in the tiny chamber, the crunch of sheep bones beneath me along with big spongy patches of what felt like moss. I looked down and could see big blue shiny beetles crawling all over the floor and among the bones.

As I shone my torch around I found several large crevices containing bird skeletons, looking like the choughs I had just seen outside, as well as an egg shell and many big shiny black spiders, with webs and silk cocoons. I also noticed that the ledge I had just crawled over seemed to be man-made, perhaps constructed by the hermit priest I had heard about?

As I squatted there I tried to meditate and tune in to get some information about this place, but it was not easy, given the surroundings, so instead I decided to try to contact the spirit of the dead sheep.

As she lay there she asked me what I wanted and as I spoke to her she answered me in a deep voice, she told me: "Go above the cave, not inside."

I apologised for disturbing her corpse and stepping all over her, and with relief I made my way back outside.

I was happy to be back in the sunlight again and breathing the fresh sea air! I stepped back from the cave entrance and surveyed the scene. Above the cave, where I had just been crawling, was a huge white granite boulder, glittering with crystals in the sunlight. It made an impressive sight!

I decided that it was time to activate the crystal I had just found, so I held it in my hand and focused on it. What I expected to happen, and what I had been taught by Alphedia, was that white light would slowly fill the crystal and then spread around my whole body until I and the crystal became one, but instead what happened was more like a nuclear explosion!

White light instantly burst forth in all directions, spreading out to the horizon in a huge burst of energy.

"Wow! This is some crystal!" I thought.

I climbed to the top of the huge granite boulder, directly above the hollow cave, and placed my newly found crystal on top of it.

A massive amount of energy instantly shot down from the sky in a column of white light and entered the boulder.

I had never felt anything like this before! It felt like this was a place of great power and that I had just reactivated it! Somehow I had been guided to perform this and had awakened an ability that I did not even know I possessed. I was not aware of it at the time but this talent would become central to my quest, yet somehow it felt like more than a gift, it was my spiritual calling!

I left the cave area and climbed up to the top of the hill, before exploring the rest of the island with its rocky shoreline and hidden bays. I walked all around the island and then watched a colony of seals playing and squabbling as I waited for the boatman to take me back to the mainland.

I arrived back on the Llyn peninsular and later on drove up to a remote headland to watch the sun go down over the magical island of Ynnis Enli.

I later found out that dowsers sometimes fix quartz crystals to standing stones in order to amplify their power. Is that what I had just done? "Perhaps the cave has been energised and should now be revisited?" I thought, "But perhaps that is for others to do and not me..."

Pudding Pie Hill, Fairy Mound

3rd November

Local folklore states that if you run around Pudding Pie Hill in Yorkshire nine times sunwise and then stick a knife in the top you will be able to hear the fairies revelling inside the mound below. Well the mound was not far from where I lived so of course I had to give it a go!

Nowadays the mound lies in the neglected corner of a field near a busy bypass, but despite this it still has quite a magical atmosphere.

I started making my way clockwise around the mound but it was not easy as it was muddy and one side of the mound ran into a hedge and ditch, but I persevered and tried not to lose count and eventually reached nine (I think!) then ran to the top and plunged my hazel wand into the soft earth. I placed my ear against the ground and heard... nothing! Perhaps I hadn't done it right, or perhaps the fairies had left here long ago, annoyed by all the busy traffic. So I sat there on top of the mound, my legs astride the implanted wand, and meditated. But try as hard as I might I could not tune in and pick anything up.

Despairing I opened my eyes, and there on my leg I saw a perfect little two-spot ladybird. Well it was not what I had come here for, but maybe it had a message for me...

He told me that his name was Azimoth and he was here to guide me. He said I had to heal the land by drawing in 'life-force' at nodal points. The land will become wasteland without this life-force to fight pollution. My work with the land is all-important, all else is just a distraction to me.

As usual it felt like a riddle. What nodal points? How do I 'heal the land'? But more than this I could not ascertain.

I tried to place Azimoth back on the ground, but he didn't seem to want to leave and so joined me as I returned to my car. As I sat behind the wheel I noticed him crawl away into my car, but after that I never saw him again.

I later discovered that an 'Azimuth' is something used in navigation. It is the angle between a point of reference and the place you want to get to. Was this a clue as to how I could find these 'nodal points'?

Tarn Hole, The Wild Man of the Woods

4th November

My research into the Hobs of North Yorkshire brought me next to Tarn Hole, a small, remote valley off the Eastern side of Bilsdale in the North York Moors. Nothing is known about the Tarn Hole Hob apart from his name but I thought I'd visit the area just to see if I could discover anything.

I drove deep into the valley down a farm track and when I had gone as far as I could go I parked up in the woods by Tarn Hole Beck.

I continued on foot up the dale, following the riverbank past large boulders left there by the ice age, and past old gnarly oak trees interspersed with bracken. The riverbank soon rose to quite a height and I soon found myself creeping along the edge of a deep gully with the river gurgling far below.

After a while the gully became less deep and looking down I could see a beautiful little glade by the river, with a tiny waterfall.

I scrambled down and found the place to be totally enchanting. A place of high energy where I could recharge my batteries. This was not a place that needed healing, it was a place that could heal me!

I felt a great urge to connect totally with this place and so I stripped off until I was completely naked and went bathing in the icy cold water.

I bathed in a pool by the waterfall and then followed the river downstream, scrambling over rocks and sliding down small cascades while all the time I could see, hear and feel the rushing water all around me.

About a hundred yards downstream I came to a muddy, gritty riverbank. I scraped out some of the mud with my fingers and started rubbing it into my arms, then my chest and pretty soon I was covered all over in mud! I wanted to mask the smells of the modern world, the shampoo, the deodorant, and become at one with this place. I started to feel like a wild man, a primitive, living in the deep forest. I rooted through the leaf litter and soon I was covered in twigs and dead leaves too. I felt like the Green Man!

I understood now what it really meant to be the Green Man; he was the wild man... the Wild Man of the Woods!

I started to tune in now in a way I never had done before. I felt like I was at one with all the vibrations of nature all around me. It felt so vibrant and alive! Not peaceful and quiet, like we imagine on a Sunday stroll, but buzzing with electricity! Everything around me was alive, really alive! It was humming and interacting in a way that is unimaginable to one who has not experienced it. Somehow everything was connected, sight, smell, hearing and the static hum that connected all things.

If this was the way that wild animals felt then it was no wonder they had such sharp instincts and could detect people approaching long before we could detect them!

I could just imagine what a clumsy, discordant note modern humans must sound when they come clumping around these forests with their big rubber-soled boots and trivial conversation. How completely disconnected from what is really going on here!

I realised then the importance of becoming connected with your own patch of Earth. To truly connect you must bring nothing in from outside. Eat only what you can gather there, clothe yourself and shelter yourself using only what you find there, only then will you be able to connect fully and truly feel like you're a part of the land.

It was an awakening, a peak experience where I felt at one with the land and with everything around me. I was tuned into the land and to the spirits, and I felt like a whole new layer of reality had been revealed to me.

Now that I had found this special place I would return again, to discover more of its magic and connect again with the raw spirits of nature.

Lindsaylands Fairy Mound (First Visit)

7th December

The next time I went to visit Alphedia she took me to a fairy mound she had just discovered. So we walked over there with her husband Auraengus to investigate.

The wooded mound was in the grounds of a country house. It was a long hogsback shape and was topped by three large beech trees and a small folly of a Greek temple.

Alphedia stepped forward and made an offering of honey in a scallop shell there beneath the most imposing of the beech trees. Auraengus and I closed our eyes and tuned in to what was going on, and then we stepped forward too...

We were immediately surrounded by tall, slim, imposing beings in white robes with a serene air about them. These were the trooping faeries, known in Gaelic as the Sidhe (pronounced Shee). Alphedia was speaking to them, but I don't remember what she was saying as at that moment I was approached by a rather flamboyant looking male Fae wearing a lace-fringed shirt. He had long, straight, dark hair and eyes that were upturned at the corners. He took me aside and gave me information that was for my ears alone.

"I am Atheron", he said, "I will be your guide. You are a faery-friend. You work for us and you will work alone. You must collect some crystals to plant."

He took out a silver necklace hung with a large, blue, tear-drop-shaped gem and hung it around my neck.

"You will get one of these for real", he told me, "Wear it with white clothes to show that you are a lightworker. When your work is done you will be rewarded. Your fairy-maiden awaits."

That was all he would tell me for now.

Alphedia was still performing her ritual so I joined her again. It seemed right to keep this information to myself for now. He had specifically told me to work alone, and Alphedia was busy pursuing so many other avenues that would just be a distraction to me.

When Alphedia was done we left the mound.

My guide Atheron accompanied me until we reached the exit between two tall trees and then I could not see him anymore.

Alphedia told me that there would be a gathering here at the winter solstice where clans of Sidhe from many raths (fairy mounds) would meet. This was going to be a very special winter solstice with a full moon and a total lunar eclipse!

It seemed like at last I had a mission, but as usual it left me with more questions than answers. What crystals should I use? Where should I plant them? The only answer I could get was that I would be guided. Why did they consider me a faery-friend? And who was this faery-maiden??

Answers to these questions would be revealed to me slowly over the coming months and years, and my understanding of them would one day change my whole perception of myself and of the world around me...

Hood Hill, Faery Fort

11th December

Hood Hill juts out from the edge of the North York Moors and makes an imposing sight when viewed from cliffs above Sutton Bank.

Legend has it that the Druids used to make sacrifices on an altar atop Hood Hill, and now somehow I felt drawn to the place.

I parked near the bottom of the hill on a cold December day and headed up through the conifer woods using my intuition to guide me in the right direction. I scrambled uphill through the trees until I reached a small clearing about halfway up the hill, and there I found what looked like an altar stone.

I left an offering by the stone and tuned in...

A female faery drifted into the clearing and told me to continue up the hill.

I made my way up through the dense spruce forest plantation until I reached a more open area near the top of the hill. This was more natural, with oak trees dotted around, waiting like sentinels for the time to come when they could spread out over the surrounding land once again. I gave them some healing with the intention that they would one day grow strong and repopulate the land below.

I continued along the hilltop until I approached the highest point on the hill where ancient earthworks were marked on my OS (Ordinance Survey) map. I was faced by what looked like bank and ditch enclosing a circular area right on the crest of the hill. Small steps had been set into the bank and beside them sat a large boulder that seemed to be guarding the entrance.

I left an offering by the stone, lit a candle, and asked permission to enter.

The faery woman reappeared and beckoned me onwards into the ring fort.

I entered the fort and then climbed to the top of the hill where a large sycamore tree stood.

The views all around were stunning! Fields and hedgerows dusted with snow stretched away to the West across the Vale of York, while away to the East lay the imposing cliffs of White Mare Crags that guarded the flanks of the North York Moors.

I stood in front of the sycamore tree, on the highest point of the hill, and planted the pointed end of my hazel wand into the ground. I then felt like the crystal I had found in Merlin's cave in Wales needed to be placed on top of it. (This crystal should be attached to my wand!)

As I did so a beam of white light shot out in all directions from the crystal. It felt like I had drawn energy into this place and then transmitted it outwards. I sat under the sycamore tree and was met by my faery guide Atheron. He told me the faeries here were pleased by what I'd done. The noble people here have been isolated for a long time, but they could now come to the solstice gathering! He then told me that I should go next to Lake Gormire to call upon and heal the water spirits there with a smooth white pebble.

I remembered then that I had collected just such a stone from the seal people (the selkies) when I was in Findhorn. I had named it my 'selkie stone.'

Atheron asked me if there's anything I would like in return. It felt like a test, so not wanting to appear greedy I told him that I'd just like to meet some of the animals of the forest.

On my way back I was greeted by the sight of three roe deer, whose prancing reminded me to be more happy and carefree. Then I was passed by a small group of long-tailed tits whose shrill whistles could be heard in the trees all around me.

As usual the information I was getting was puzzling and cryptic, but I was learning to just go along with it, and not to expect too many answers. Sometimes the tasks I had to perform seemed so small and simple that it left me thinking there must be more to it; but somehow I felt that I was transferring energies around from place to place, and perhaps that was all that was required of me at that time.

Lake Gormire is very near to Hood Hill and so I could return to perform my task there the very next day.

Lake Gormire, Awakening the Dragon

12th December

Lake Gormire is an Ice-Age lake, tucked away behind its glacial moraine (an earthern bank pushed up by the ice during the last ice-age). It lies just beneath the western edge of the North York Moors. The lake had always intrigued me; it is semi-circular in shape, and yet entirely natural. It is said that an ancient village lies buried beneath the waters, which can sometimes be glimpsed on a clear day and the sound of its church bells can be heard.

At the faery rath on Hood Hill the day before, I had got the message to go to Lake Gormire to, "Call upon and heal the spirits of the lake with a smooth white pebble". So I brought the smooth white pebble that I had picked up in the bay at Findhorn, the one I called my 'selkie stone'.

The air was cold and frosty as I parked my car in a lane at the far side of the lake and then slipped and slid down an icy path through the woods until I reached the lakeside. There I got a bit of a shock... the entire lake was frozen solid! In Yorkshire that's quite an unusual sight, as rarely does it get so cold as to freeze over a lake of this size, and there had been a thaw for several days previously.

I placed my pebble on the frozen edge of the lake and called upon the selkies.

I had a vision of naked women with long flowing hair gliding over the lake towards me. At the very bottom of the lake, deep down at the bottom of a cone-shaped depression, I could sense an awesome and powerful presence. I sensed the form of a sleeping dragon!

I planted my wand into the snow at the edge of the lake, attached the crystal, and then called upon the spirits of the place to awaken:

"Selkies of the lake,
Dragon of the lake,
Spirit of the lake,
Awake!"

I cast the pebble out onto the lake and it slid across the frozen surface until it skidded to a halt in the snow.

The female water spirits were drawn to the pebble and began to dance around it and draw energy from it. They span around and around it until they transformed into a cone that rose into the air like a whirlwind. The selkies could still be seen dancing in the rushing cone of air as it extended all the way up into the sky, and down to the very bowels of the lake, connecting heaven with earth.

I suddenly felt compelled to join them and so I took a tentative step onto the edge of the frozen lake. But how thick was the ice? Could it hold my weight? Who could rescue me if it cracked and I fell in? Isn't this what water spirits do? Lure people to their deaths?

I slid my other foot forward slowly and the ice began to sing as it adjusted to my weight! Waves of sound rippling across it like a sheet of metal being flexed. Having previously lived in the frozen wastes of Scandinavia I was not too disturbed by this as I was familiar with the sound, but I slid forward even more gingerly after that surprise. Step by step I slowly made my way forward, I could sense stirrings deep in the lake below me. The dragon could rise up and consume me at any moment! I would never be seen again...

After what seemed like an age I finally reached the pebble far out in the lake, I could sense the depth of the water beneath me which at any other time of the year would have swallowed me up and consumed me. Only a thin layer of ice now protected me from the unknown depths. I was walking where none were meant to walk; but I soon settled down and tuned back in to what was going on.

The female spirits were still dancing in their cone and chanting:

*"We dance for energy,
For happiness,
For joy,
For life!"*

I joined them in their dance and span round and round. I became part of their whirling cone that connected the sky with the earth dragon below, drawing down energy and sending it deep into the bowels of the lake. The dragon stirred and cast up bubbles from his nostrils. We had awakened him!

In that moment I felt like my task was completed and so I took up my stone and slid back to the lake side. I reached the snow-covered earth with a great sigh of relief!

I then set off walking around the lake and soon heard a gentle trickling sound ahead. I had read that the lake had no outlets or inlets so I was surprised by this. As I approached the trickling sound it suddenly stopped! So I searched around and found a small wet outlet that seemed to disappear underground, but I couldn't catch a sound of the trickling again. I remembered reading a folk tale about a goose that disappeared through one of these holes and was later found miles away without any feathers! Was this perhaps the place from that story?

As I turned back to the path I was startled to notice a large circle of melted ice far out on the lake which I'm sure hadn't been there before! Was this the dragon's breath causing the ice to melt?

I continued around the lake, viewing it from all sides, struggling along the icy paths through the woods until I reached my starting point again, and then for some reason felt compelled to circle the entire lake another two times!

Feeling quite exhausted I finally completed my thrice sunwise circuit and sat down. I felt that there was still more to do here and so I sent my awareness out into the lake.

I felt my spirit, or avatar, take on the form of a large, muscular, horned being made from pure white light. He strode out onto the lake and stood over the melted ring of ice, plunged his arms into the water and hauled on a huge chain. He pulled and pulled with all his might until a dragon's head emerged from the water, attached to the other end of the chain! He held on to the dragon using all his strength, I could feel him straining at the chain and knew he wouldn't be able to hold him for too long.

I picked up my crystal-tipped wand and pointed it at the dragon.

A burst of energy immediately shot out from the dragon and sent a beam of light all the way to the top of Hood Hill. I had a vision of the beam of energy striking my quartz crystal that had been there the day before and then spreading out in all directions. Perhaps the beams of energy were connecting to other similar places, forming a network of energy lines all over the land? My avatar then let go of the chain and the dragon sank back into the depths of the lake. My work here was done at last.

Well I cannot say that it had not been an eventful day... what an experience! But what was I doing exactly? Creating ley lines?? Somehow the energy of this earth dragon was being used to charge up the spot where I had placed my crystal on Hood Hill. This energy grid connecting the fairy forts together certainly seemed to be something important. Was this then my task? Only time would tell...

Lindsaylands Fairy Mound (Second visit)

15th December

After my first visit to the fairy mound in Lindsaylands I was told by the Fae to collect some crystals. I wasn't told which crystals to collect, just that I should use my intuition to guide me. With this in mind I visited a large crystal wholesalers in Yorkshire and was immediately drawn to the green fluorite, which were green crystals with purple inclusions, and some of them were formed into the shape of small eggs. So I bought these along with several other crystals. (I later learned that green fluorite had an association with the faeries, so my intuition had been spot on!).

I returned to Scotland on a cold December morning and immediately went back to visit the faery mound.

I could see my guide Atheron there, the tall, dark-haired fae I had met on my first visit, and he led me back to the great beech tree on top of the long mound.

I felt drawn to give some energy to this tree so I closed my eyes and placed my hands against the trunk.

I could feel the energy passing from my hand, coursing through trunk, branch, root and twig to fill the entire tree with healing light.

I was starting to realise that I really had this power to heal and to

impart energy where it was required!
I opened my eyes and was astounded to see all the moss covering the tree glowing a vivid green, the colour was so bright and intense that everything seemed lucid and magical, more real and intense than everyday reality ever was. The green sheen that covers most of the tree is barely visible normally.

I closed my eyes again and this time travelled with Atheron deep inside the tree to meet the faery king. He stood there with his court and came to greet me like an old friend, which indeed I was, as I could suddenly remember having visited this place many times before in long ages past. Somehow I felt like I was one of them, one of these noble race of beings. I looked down and saw that I was wearing a white shirt of silky appearance and on my chest sparkled an intense blue teardrop shaped gem.

"Greetings Aurvandil!" he said to me as he hugged me.

Was that who I was? Aurvandil? It certainly felt like I was him now. The human being I was on Earth seemed like another person, a strange shell that I had been inhabiting, full of negative emotions. Had I forgotten my true identity in order to live as a human and carry out my task here on Earth? The faery king called himself Erowyn and as he spoke to me of the world of the fae a flood of memories came back to me, memories of a beautiful and undying land where nothing ever faded or decayed, where everything remained constant and true to its perfect form. I realised that the Fae had no wish to come back to Earth, they were content in their own land, but Earth was under attack by dark forces. The balance of nature was slowly being destroyed, and the "day of reckoning" was soon to come when mankind would have to pay back for all they had taken.

I was told to take my twelve green fluorite eggs and to plant them in the Earth like seeds; to return to Hood Hill and start my task there, planting my crystal-tipped wand into the ground once more to bring energy into these locations, but more than that I could not ascertain, the true meaning of my quest and the meaning of the coming solstice gathering still eluded me.

I knew that once my task was done here on Earth I would return to this Otherworld. There was a faery woman there, and she seemed very familiar to me somehow. I could see her standing in the background, and I felt a deep connection with her and I knew that one day I would return to the undying lands and be with her once more.

I was also told that dark forces were against me and would try to sabotage my mission. This included fears, doubts and suspicions that would enter into my consciousness.

I walked away from the mound with much to think about. What a revelation to suddenly remember a whole existence that I had completely forgotten! But it didn't feel strange or odd, it felt perfectly natural, like I had always known it.

I returned to the mound later to leave my fluorite eggs under the tree. They would be left there overnight and while resting there would be infused with the energies needed to complete my task.

Lunar Eclipse with the Fae

21st December - Winter Solstice

This was going to be a special day, not only was it the winter solstice, and a full moon, but it would also be a total lunar eclipse, and the day when the clans of the Fae were going to have their gathering!

The winter solstice, the shortest day of the year, is one of those magical times when the veil between our world and the Otherworld is thinnest; the night of the full moon is a time when people have commonly seen the Fae according to folklore; and the total eclipse is a time of dark magic, when normal rules do not apply!

The night before the solstice was bright and clear, and the moon, already looking full, beamed down from a clear black sky peppered with stars.

I stood and meditated under the full moon and had a vision of the Fae pushing a large cart up a hill. The cart contained a huge glowing white disc which I assumed represented the moon. The cart reached the top of the hill and hundreds of Fae were gathered around, perhaps engaging in some kind of ceremony.

For weeks now we had been getting messages that the Fae were going to gather on the solstice near to the fairy mound in Lindsaylands. It seemed like the gathering had already started, but exactly where they were and what they were doing I could not ascertain.

I got up at six o'clock the next morning in order to see the eclipse. As I stepped outside I could see that the sky was crystal clear and the moon was a glowing white ball, filling the sky with its radiance.

I drove to the fairy mound in Lindsaylands and by the time I got there I looked up through the trees and could already see that part of the moon was being eaten by the shadow of the Earth. I tuned in at the fairy mound but there were no Fae there, none at all! Were they all away performing their ceremony on a hilltop somewhere?

I decided to drive to Tinnis Castle in Merlindale to get a better view of the morning sky. I wanted to walk to the top of the hill but it was intensely cold, below -15°c and in any case the eclipse was now almost total. I did not want to miss it and so I stopped to take in the intense atmosphere as the moon entered into shadow and turned a deep red colour.

I was disappointed that I had not had any encounters with the Fae that night, and I could not work out where they were all gathered, but today was the solstice and tonight was the longest night, so there was still time...

Alphedia was running a fairy magic course in her yurt (a spacious round tent) that day to coincide with the solstice and the Fae gathering. It was icy cold but it soon warmed up inside the yurt. We did some meditations to get into the right frame of mind and connected with the four elements of earth, air, fire and water. I became one with each of the elements, like I was an elemental myself, merging with the earth, and then with the air, fire and water, feeling what it was like to become a flame or to disperse on an ocean current.

Once the light started to fade that evening we all walked over to the fairy mound, passed by the folly of a Greek temple, and stood facing the magical beech tree.

We had come in the twilight to meet the fairy king, so we left an offering of honey beneath the tree, closed our eyes, and then tuned in to the faery realm.

We saw King Erowyn and his queen seated on their thrones surrounded by their fairy court. My guide Atheron was there too, a flamboyant dark elf. We each stepped forward to receive a gift from the faery king. As I knelt down before him I had a glowing necklace of light placed around my neck and a glowing circlet of light placed on my head.

I was wearing a blue crystal and silver necklace which I had been inspired to purchase a few days earlier in imitation of my vision, and I felt the magical light enter it. But before I got chance to find out more it was time for us to leave. We were walking back at the most magical time of the evening, the deep twilight, when day vision gives way to night vision. The moon had not yet risen and a slight haziness hung in the air. Alphedia paused and turned to look at the field by the fairy mound. We all stopped to look and suddenly I saw a twinkle of light, then another, and then another! Each time coming from an entirely different part of the field, a sudden twinkle that disappeared faster than you could look at it, sometimes blue, sometimes white. I stood gazing in wonder, I had never seen anything like this before! It seemed like at the most magical time of the night on one of the most magical days of the year that anything was possible!

Alphedia soon turned and walked away, she had seen the fairy lights many times before, but I stood entranced. In addition to the twinkling fairy lights I was starting to discern faint patches of light moving back and forth across the field, like faint clouds of luminescence; but after a while I too had to pull myself away from the entrancing spectacle before I froze solid, it was a very cold night! In any case the twilight was passing and a hazy moon was just starting to rise above the trees on the opposite side of the field, banishing the twilight with its luminous glow.

We returned to the yurt and ate our fairy feast, but something was drawing me back to the mound, I felt like the day was not done yet! Sara was with us and she also wanted to return to the fairy mound and so, just before midnight, we made our way back there in the darkness and extreme cold.

I entered their realm once more and spoke some more with King Erowyn. He now called me Earendil, the wayfarer and the waymaker, and he explained to me how back in the faery realm I somehow travelled from rath to rath connecting the web and joining the points of power. I started to remember my life in the faery realm, my long travels and my warm greetings in each of the fairy forts (raths) which I seemed to visit in some kind of circuit; but it still felt like the purpose of my work in the Otherworld was beyond my comprehension, even the word 'work' seemed inappropriate, it was more like a calling, a purpose for being.

Sara was meanwhile having an experience of her own, being carried off into the stars to meet the "creator", an experience which seemed to be overwhelming for her! I had to help bring her back down to earth, we then made our way back from the dark frozen landscape to the warmth of Alphedia's cosy house.

* * *

A few days later I did some research on the internet and came up with some amazing information and connections. Aurvandil and Earendil are one and the same! Aurvandil being Norse and Earendil being Saxon, they both mean "Luminous Wanderer" and refer either to the morning star (Venus) or the star Rigel (Aurvandil's toe from Snorri's Edda).

The Anglo-Saxon poem 'Christ I' has this:

"Hail Earendil!
Brightest of angels!
Over middle-earth to men sent,
The true radiance of the sun,

Bright above the stars,
Every season thou of thyself
Ever illuminest!"

Tolkien, being a scholar of Old Norse and Anglo-Saxon, picked up on this and used the name for one of the elves in 'The Silmarillion':

"Hail Eärendil, brightest of stars!"

Eärendil carried the light of the morning star upon his brow. His jewel was a green beryl (or emerald) which was set into a silver brooch in the shape of an eagle with outspread wings. It was said that looking through the stone, one would see burned and withered things heal again, "The hand that holds it heals", he says.

Eärendil married Elwing who was forced to cast herself into the sea with one of the magical gems known as Silmarils, but she was saved by the sea god Ulmo who turned her into a great white bird.

Is Tolkien tapping into some ancient knowledge here, or did he just make it all up? It is interesting to speculate that perhaps he was somehow receiving this knowledge directly from the Otherworld. He certainly spent a long time trying to collate it all and make sense of it. He never did finish The Silmarillion but instead just left a huge pile of incredibly detailed and extensive notes, including maps, histories, genealogies and two complete Elven languages!

As well as doing some research I also got around to attaching my quartz crystal (the one I had found in Merlin's cave on Bardsey Island) to the end of my wand. Now it really felt like a powerful tool! Capable of channelling and anchoring energies. I looked forward to using it out in the field again!

Return to Hood Hill, The Dark Elves

26th December

A few days after the solstice I returned to Hood Hill with my newly energised crystals in order to find out their true purpose.

I climbed straight up the hill through the wet snow until I reached the fairy fort at the summit. Once there I placed a large quartz crystal before me and tuned in to the energies up there. I was told to place the quartz crystal in the large sycamore tree that seemed to be at the centre of the energies. I was also told to remove an electronic device which I found hanging there.

I inspected the electronic device which was hanging from the tree, it seemed to be some sort of GPS device used by an orienteering club, and it was firmly attached with thick wire. There was no way I could remove it without bolt cutters and so I took down the telephone number so I could phone the club later to tell them to come and collect their discarded device.

I then walked around the tree and inspected its trunk and branches a bit more closely. After a while I found a knotty hole which fitted my crystal perfectly. I stuck the crystal in the hole and left it jutting out like a thumb.

I was then disturbed by a local farmer out for a stroll. I got talking to him and he told me about a hidden spring and stone water trough further down the western side of the hill, so I made a mental note to go and look for it later.

After he left I turned back to my crystal. It was jutting out between a large fork in the main trunk. Either the tree had split very near to the ground, or this was two trees that had grown together. I stood there and meditated, trying to work out what to do next. Suddenly I realised that the fork in the tree was a magical gateway! I opened my eyes and all the moss was glowing a vivid green, just like it had done in Lindsaylands a few days ago.

I closed my eyes again and stepped through the gateway...

I was in a dark cavern with tall guards dressed in dark, horned armour. They led me down a passageway and there I found the dark elf king sitting behind his desk. He greeted me and I asked him what I was to do with my crystals. His answer was that I should make a grid around the moors, with one point on Hood Hill, and the opposite point on Janet's Foss in Mulgrave Woods. A large quartz crystal should then be placed in the centre of the grid, this would protect the moors from the coming pestilence!

I returned to my body on Hood Hill and thought about what he had said. I still was not sure what I really had to do. Mulgrave Woods are on the eastern side of the moor, by the sea, but where was the centre of the grid? Should I be using my fluorite eggs, or should it be quartz crystals? Did I even trust this dark elf king? Something felt strangely sinister about him and about this whole place. In any case I did not leave any crystals there that day, I felt like I had to go away and find more clarity first.

I wandered through the thick trees on the far side of the hill, and my intuition led me to very spring that the farmer had just told me about. There was something special about this spring. I felt like I would be back this way another day...

Cropton, Water Nymphs of the Lady Keld Spring

28th December

On a cold and misty day at the tail end of the year I drove to the quaint little Yorkshire moorland village of Cropton and parked my car up by the old church of St. Gregory's.

I had been drawn to Cropton by the following piece of folklore:

> *About the middle of the eighteenth century, the people of Cropton were sadly troubled by "a company of evil water elves having their abode in a certain deep spring at the high end of*

that village," and in order to rid themselves of the sprites, a most heathen ceremony was conducted at the spring, "three wenches" taking a prominent part in the proceedings which are quite unprintable.

After scouring a map of the local area, I settled upon the Lady Keld Spring as being the only likely location where this "heathen ceremony" could have taken place.

The mist hung heavy over the land as I trudged my way down through the snow-laden woods behind the church. I was following an ancient pathway that monks and pilgrims had once used on their way to visit the magical healing waters of the spring.

The air was silent and mysterious and I passed further and further down the hill, through woods and fields, until finally I could hear the sound of trickling water in the trees ahead of me, just beyond a barbed-wire fence.

As I climbed over the fence I could feel a sudden change in the energy, from the heavy stillness of the fields and woods to the crisp fresh energy of the springs. The air was buzzing and alive!

As I stepped forward I could see a central rivulet that was being fed by many small springs all around, causing a lively flow of water to pass through the deep snow.

I knelt down and left an offering there by the water, and suddenly found myself saying:

"Fair maidens of the Lady Spring,
A humble gift I for thee bring,
With words of hope and healing hand,
I call thee forth across this land!"

“Where did that come from?!” I wondered. I had never been much into poetry before...

I decided to follow the rivulet upstream, as clearly there must be more springs above that were feeding it. The snow was deep but the spring water was cutting through it to leave dark patches in the snow wherever a little spring or rivulet appeared. Despite the ice and frost all around, this lively spring water did not look like it was about to freeze up. Eventually though I came upon a large frozen pond. It felt like a significant place and so I drew forth my wand.

The quartz crystal on the tip of my wand shone, casting a halo of white light all around it. The halo spread out until it was several yards wide and I then swept the edge of the halo over the frozen surface of the water until eventually the crystal itself was pointing directly into the heart of the pool. A shaft of pure white light beamed out from the crystal and penetrated the ice, entering the water's hidden depths. Energy was being transferred into the water, creating a vortex.

I could see small glowing creatures about a foot long flitting about under the ice, anthropomorphic figures with mermaid's tails, like little water sprites. They swam from the edges of the pool towards the vortex in the centre and seemed to swirl around it, bathing in its energy.

The white light from my wand eventually filled the whole pool and then seemed to pass down the rivulet and into all the springs in this hidden little valley. More sprites emerged from the springs where they had been sleeping and hiding from the world, they passed down into the rivulet and in a glowing torrent of sparkling bodies passed out into the wider world.

I now felt like I needed to anchor this energy, but my wand would not stick into the ice, so I stuck it into a small patch of turf that rose above the surface of the pool.

I felt energy pass from the wand and into the earth there.

Walking around the pool I then discovered that the rivulet continued even further upstream, so I followed it until I came to another pool. This pool was not completely frozen over like the first one but was matted with bright green pond weeds.

I drew forth my wand and prepared to repeat the process I had carried out on the first pond, but this time the result was quite different!

Three naked women emerged from the water. They beckoned me in a tempting way, but occasionally I would catch a glimpse of them looking like old hags, with sharp pointed teeth and pond weeds in their hair. Were these the "Jenny Greenteeth" of folklore that lured men to their deaths?

I sent white healing light towards them with my wand. I saw their shadow sides being driven out and sent skyward. Had I dispelled these evil spirits? The now beautiful nymphs approached me and started stroking me.

"We would have of thee! We would have of thee Aurvandil!" they hissed.

I could still see flashes of malice in their eyes but they were beautiful and tempting! They led me into the water and then slowly down under the water to their watery home. At the last moment I snapped out of my trance and broke free! I swam back to the surface and climbed up onto the bank.

"Fare thee well then Aurvandil!" they said.

One of them tossed me a golden ring which I caught in my hand. They said that the ring would protect me so I placed it on my finger. Did this mean I could use it to call upon these water nymphs in future?

I was left wondering about this as I walked back up the hill towards the village. Did I just have a lucky escape or was Aurvandil immune to their magic? It was certainly an interesting experience in any case! And I seemed to be doing some good work by bringing the positive energy of the water sprites back into the land.

Back in the village I paid a visit to Cropton's other famous water supply, a three hundred foot deep well in the centre of the main street.

Did this well too have sprites and magic lurking within it? I did not detect anything at this time, and in any case the local villagers were now eyeing me suspiciously so I wandered back to the church. I had a look around inside and found a leaflet about a nearby crypt beneath the church at Lastingham, an ancient sacred site full of old Saxon and Viking stonework and said to be the centre of many ley lines and strange phenomena. It seemed like a place I would soon have to visit! By this time twilight was fast approaching and something drew me back to the medieval trackway beside the church. I was sure that there must be Fae associated with this place. Behind the church was an old Norman motte which I had missed earlier. I walked up and climbed it, then from the top gazed out into the mist. I half expected the Fae to appear from the twilight at any moment, but I saw nothing.

I wandered back across the field beside the motte and soon found myself walking back through the woods towards the Lady Keld Spring. I crossed the barbed-wire fence once more and the fresh, clean energy of the springs hit me again! What a difference! One side of the fence felt heavy and still, while the other side was sparkling with energy!

I stood with my feet on either side of the rivulet, soaking up the energy of the place, letting it invigorate me! The trickling water passed beneath me and the sparkling energy electrified the air all around me. I closed my eyes and suddenly found myself gushing in rhyme again!

"I come to thee to set thee free,
Along the road to what may be,
I've travelled down to misty dell,
To learn the secrets of the well,
To take them with me far away,
To use in earnest one fine day!"

Not prize winning poetry by any means, but how was this rhyme coming spontaneously to my lips without me even thinking about it?

As I pondered this I was startled by a sudden sound... I opened my eyes and saw two roe deer leap over the barbed-wire fence just feet away from where I had crossed it. They landed just a few yards from me and sniffed the air. They had not seen me! I stood perfectly still over the stream in the twilight, hardly daring to breath. My leg started to cramp up as I watched the uncertainty in the deer's face. She had sensed something but she was not sure... we all stood there in perfect silence until the lead deer suddenly made a decision and started to walk, straight towards me! At the last moment she noticed me and leapt backwards into the air! They then both shot off in the other direction as fast as their agile limbs could carry them!

At last I could relax. What an exhilarating experience! Well I had not seen any Fae this night but this had been just as magical. Nature is truly awe inspiring!

As I walked back up the hill in the darkness some doubts started to creep in. Maybe I had missed an opportunity? Maybe the deer wanted to communicate with me? I had been been too overawed to think about it at the time though. As I walked back through the forest, owls hooted at each other in the darkness. No, nature goes on regardless of us I thought, our concerns are not theirs.

Baysdale, Fairies Butter Wasing

1st January

Folklore states that in Baysdale on the North York Moors there is a spring where the fairies wash their 'fairy butter'. I did some research on the internet and found out that fairy butter is a kind of fungus, it gets its name from the fact that it seems to appear miraculously overnight on gate posts and fences and looks like a blob of butter that the fairies have been throwing at each other during the hours of darkness.

Baysdale lies in a forgotten corner of the North York Moors, it is accessible only by a farm track and it is all private land, there are no public facilities, not even a layby to park in. I realised that my presence there would arouse suspicion from the local farmers so I tried to make myself as inconspicuous as possible, parking behind a low mound on the entrance road that led down into the hidden valley.

I walked down the hill and headed for the cover of the nearest forest and soon found myself in a magical birch wood. It felt like a very high energy place, almost untouched by the outside world.

I stood in a clearing in the birch forest and communed with the birch spirits there; tall, thin, stick-like beings that peeked out from behind the trees. I sent them healing with my wand but also soaked up some the magical energy of this place for myself too. The birch people thanked me and said that if I ever needed their help, all I had to do was find a birch tree!

I walked up onto the moor behind the forest and found some boggy springs seeping out of the ground. I had no clue as to where to go but I knew that this wasn't the right place, the spring I was looking for would probably be gushing out of the rocks, not seeping out of the hillside. It would be the kind of spring that people in the past could visit and fetch water.

I continued walking around the edge of the dale (valley) until I reached the far end, and then headed back down into the dale through a conifer plantation. Soon I could hear the unmistakable sound of trickling water! I followed the sound through fallen trees and low-hanging branches and eventually found its source, bubbling forth from between some rocks.

Although it was heavily clogged with fallen leaves I instinctively knew that this was the right place! The withered trees growing out of the rocks nearby and the odd birch tree still clinging on to life gave clues as to what this place must have looked like in the past before the conifer plantation grew up; and despite the shadow cast by those suffocating trees looming overhead it still held some of its ancient magic.

Immediately above the spring I could see tiny caverns, no more than a foot high, sheltered under overhanging boulders. I was drawn to go and inspect them closer and then sat down by one of the entrances and meditated. I took out my wand, pointed the crystal into the hole and sent healing rays deep down inside.

After a while small, shy faces peeked out of the holes. They belonged to tiny creatures about 8-10 inches tall with brown skin, long slanted eyes, and long pointy brown ears. They stood on two legs and wore simple rustic clothing.

I planted my wand into the ground before me and the crystal on its tip glowed. Cautiously the little 'boggles' crept out and formed a circle all around me. They then linked hands and formed two concentric circles facing me in the centre and started to dance; one circle dancing clockwise while the other circle danced anti-clockwise. They sang:

"HEY LEE lap-ehay!"
"HEY LEE lap-ehay!"

They seemed to be performing some kind of festive ritual or celebration. I felt like it was time to reveal my true form as Aurvandil, the faery lord in glowing white. As I did so they stopped dancing and cautiously stepped forward, they seemed to want to touch me in awe, like I was some kind of living god.

I told them that they did not need to hide anymore, their time was come, they could spread out now and meet with others of their kind. They all came up and touched me before slowly melting away back into the rock crevices and undergrowth from whence they had come.

I returned to my body and picked up my wand and then wandered back down to the spring. As I peered into the water I got a surprise... fungus? Fairy butter!

I had never seen fungus under water before, I did not even know such a thing was possible! I picked up the fungus, it wasn't attached to anything. Had the fairies been washing their fairy butter? For what strange purpose did they perform this task? That would have to remain a mystery, but I was more than happy to find this confirmation of my quest.

Hecate and the Fairy Cross Plain

2nd January

Earlier in the year I had met an old druidess who heard some of my story and informed me that I should be working with the goddess Hecate. I did not feel entirely comfortable with that as I associated Hecate with the darker side of magic and witchcraft; but when the festival of Samhain came around last year I felt like it was an appropriate time to try to contact the goddess.

I had cast a magic circle in my room and then summoned the goddess by name.

She appeared but would not answer any of my questions directly. She told me to meet her instead at the crossroads by "The Old Hell Way".

I did not sleep very well that night, wondering what else I may have summoned through the dark portal that I had opened in my room.

The Old Hell Way I had already heard about; it was a spirit road on the North York Moors where in the past corpses were carried from Fryupdale, over Danby Rigg, to the old church in Danby. The crossroads she was referring to lay on the Fairy Cross Plain, an area steeped in fairy lore and surely a crossing place of old spirit roads in times gone by. I had read the folklore about these spirit roads, how the ghosts of the dead could be seen marching down them, and sometimes the fairies too. Were fairy paths the same as spirit roads? Did the fairies and the dead inhabit the same realm? Or was it all just a trick played by the fairies to fool people with their shape-shifting? Either way I intended to visit the Fairy Cross Plain and find out.

* * *

I arrived at the crossroads by the Old Hell Way late in the afternoon. The weather was freezing cold and a light dusting of snow covered the land. I could see the Old Hell Way snaking up the hillside to my left, but my attention was drawn to a curious looking rounded hill away to my right. As soon as I saw it I thought, "That's a fairy hill!" It sat right in the middle of the Fairy Cross Plain.

I decided to explore the Old Hell Way first and started ploughing up through snow that was knee deep in places.

As I passed along the ancient trackway I envisioned ghostly processions marching by, a land of the dead imprinted upon the earth, spectral forms from times gone by.

It felt uncomfortable and I had read that spirit roads were places best avoided due to the unhealthy energies that passed along them. I wanted to see some of the standing stones that marked this ancient path over the rigg but soon the snow was up to my thighs so I decided that to continue on was pointless. In any case dusk was fast approaching so I made my way back down. Along the way I heard eerie voices coming from the moor, and then the sudden sounds of red grouse crowing and flapping their wings in the failing light.

I arrived back at the crossroads and decided that I could put it off no longer, it was time to contact Hecate.

I tuned in to the misty, dusk-laden landscape and there she appeared, looking tall, lithe and sensuous in a long, flowing dress of midnight black. I welcomed her, the "dark goddess", but she corrected me instantly as, turning, she revealed her bright white side. Half black and half white was her face, but whether she represented good and evil, or winter and summer I could not say.

"Why did you want to meet me here?" I asked.

"It was not by your will that you came here but by the will of others," she replied.

I thought of the druidess who had led me to contact Hecate. Had it all been a mistake then? Should I have been listening to my own intuition and not to the guidance of others?

"Your mission lies with the fairies of the cross plain," she said. "Climb the hill, place your crystal there, then all will be revealed!" and with that she disappeared.

As usual I was left with more questions than answers, and feeling no wiser than I had done before. By now it was dark so I decided that I would return to investigate the fairy hill in the morning.

* * *

The hill was indicated on local maps as "Round Hill" but its prominent location, right in the middle of the basin known as the Fairy Cross Plain belied its prosaic name. Sure enough, a little investigation soon revealed that it was indeed once known as "Fairy Hill"!

I approached this time from a different direction, which gave an even better view of the Fairy Cross Plain and the prominent location of the Fairy Hill. Away and to the right I could clearly make out the Old Hell Way winding its way up Danby Rigg.

I parked in a lane near the hill and climbed over a fence into the boggy field. As I approached the slope of the hill I found an old spring that was being utilised by the local farmer.

I made a mental note of this important feature and continued on around the hill. I didn't walk straight to the top but spiralled around, checking out its slopes that seemed to be littered with a whole honeycomb of rabbit warrens, the rabbits scurrying away in all directions at my approach and disappearing inside the hill. It felt like the rabbits were guardians, but guardians of what? A grassy knoll in a windswept valley?

I reached the top of the hill and planted my wand firmly in its crown.

Instantly I could see the crystal shining, and playful elfin spirits seemed to materialise from all around and started to dance a crazy carefree dance around and around my wand. They were human sized creatures with naked, shiny brown skin, long black slanted eyes and sharply pointed ears. They seemed to be mindlessly playful and joyous, caring about nothing, strangely alien and incomprehensible.

The grinning face of a dancing elf approached me: "We dance around the fairy ring, but you shall not see our faery king!" he squawked.

They took hold of my hands and got me to dance with them, but I had to stop before I went crazy like them!

"I wish to meet your king!" I said. "I bring gifts from King Erowyn."

"We would know what you do bring, before you meet the fairy king!" he said in a most sarcastically playful voice.

I took the fluorite eggs from my pouch, the same ones I had left on the faery mound in Lindsaylands to be energised by the fairies there. I felt like I must lay them out as if they were the points of a twelve pointed star, with six outer crystals forming a larger star, and six inner crystals interspersed between them, forming a smaller star inside.

It was then that I realised my mistake! I had only ten eggs!

At that moment the king appeared, an old sage-like man with white hair and a bushy beard. He wore a long, richly decorated cloak and carried a long staff in one hand.

"I bring some beryls, shiny green, fit for faery king or queen!" I said.

Had I made another mistake? These were not beryls! In any case the king looked jovial enough and greeted me warmly. I apologised to him for the missing two gems:

"My lord I do not mean thee ill, take these stones for my goodwill!"

I promised him that I would leave these ten stones here, and return with the other two as soon as I could. I found a suitable abandoned rabbit hole nearby and placed the stones deep inside, away from prying eyes.

I bid goodbye to the king and stepped off down the hill. I saw more rabbits scurrying away and started to wonder about them some more. I knelt by one of the rabbit holes and decided to take a spirit journey inside.

Deeper and deeper I went into the maze of warrens inside the hill until I reached the very centre, and there in the middle was the most enormous crystal I had ever seen, a quartz point as tall as a building! So this was the secret that the rabbits were guarding! It was almost as if the whole hill had been built in ancient times, just to hide this crystal. Truly this was a place of hidden power!

It would take me a couple of months before I could organise more fluorite crystals and go to Scotland to get them energised, but I would return...

Roulston Scar and the Devil's Parlour

24th January

Roulston Scar forms a headland of limestone cliffs on the southwestern edge of the North York Moors, a continuation of the Whitestone cliffs near Sutton Bank. To the eastern side lies the famous Kilburn white horse, carved into the hillside during the nineteenth century, while above the cliffs sits an airfield where gliders regularly cast off into the void between Roulston Scar and Hood Hill, and glide on the thermal air currents that flow up the cliff face. But I was not here to watch aerial displays, I was here to find a hidden cave in the cliff face that was known in local folklore as the Devil's Parlour. I had no idea however if the cave even existed.

The cliffs of Roulston Scar are high and their base sits upon very steep wooded slopes which are inaccessible without climbing and scrambling. The cliffs run west from the white horse, and then curve around to the northeast as they head towards Sutton Bank to form a kind of a headland that projects out over a densely wooded valley that separates Roulston Scar from Hood Hill.

I decided to start near the white horse and make my way along the cliff top, but I hadn't gone very far before I noticed strangely perforated rocks set into the steep hillside below me. I was intrigued and decided to give the rocks a closer inspection, so I scrambled down the hillside and climbed over them, inspecting the large cup-shaped depressions that seemed to have been gouged out of them.

I climbed further down and was amazed to see a whole row of these huge boulders that seemed to have cavities carved out of them everywhere which gave them the appearance of a giant Swiss cheese.

I shone my torch inside and could see a whole honeycomb of tiny caverns and passageways, like some subterranean world that had been carved out by mysterious small hands.

I sat down there and tuned in, and suddenly I could see them! Tiny 'boggles' about 8 inches tall with brown furry skin and long, pointy drooping ears. They each wore rustic-looking breeches with braces passing over their shoulders.

At first they were afraid, peering out from dark corners of their subterranean caverns, but again I surprised myself by starting to talk in rhyme. I spoke long with them, too much to recall this time, asking them to come out and sing and play and have no fear. Having gotten over their initial mistrust, all of a sudden they started to sing: "Hey-hey-yap! Hey-hey-yap!" and slowly they crept out into the light.

Soon they were dancing around and playing and climbing all over me. They knew then that I had come to liberate them! I planted my wand firmly in the ground and white light shone forth from it, illuminating all the dark places within the rocks.

I drew in energy and concentrated it into my hands which started to glow red. One by one the boggles leaped forward and touched my glowing hands, each one taking a little bit of the fiery energy for itself before returning to the rock and carrying the energy to its own little cavern which then seemed to glow red also with the energy that had been brought back. It seemed then that every cavern turned into a little forge, where happy little boggles were beating away joyously forging magical metalware.

I could sense now that the whole ridge seemed to have come back to life and was filled with energy. The tiny boggles were everywhere!

I edged further along the ridge, climbing through the undergrowth, and passed many more of these pock-marked rocks along the way.

Some of the holes looked truly bizarre, like dinosaur eggs that had just hatched, while others looked like they had been deliberately broken into, chipped at and mined. For what purpose? And by whom? Were the boggles mining for hidden treasures?

The whole ridge seemed to be buzzing with energy now, and I felt like my job had been done. I was about to leave the steep slope behind and scramble back up to the cliff top when I heard a woodpecker drumming at a tree in the forest below me and then saw a flash of red and black as he flew further down the slope. I had heard it was lucky to follow woodpeckers, so I decided that I had to follow this one too to see where it would lead me.

I scrambled down the steep muddy slope, past stunted ancient oak trees that had rarely seen the passage of man, and followed animal tracks through dense thorn bushes until eventually I came to a clearing where there were rocks smothered in bright green ivy. I stopped and looked around. It was a magical place! Untouched by the outside world which was so close by, yet protected by its inaccessible location.

I had travelled west slightly, across the cliff face, and was now facing uphill towards an ivy-covered boulder. To the left of the boulder was a forked tree, and beyond it a small glade that seemed even more magical. I knew this was a special place. I closed my eyes and took a step through the forked tree, but a voice in my head told me to leave my backpack and coat behind. I dropped them to the ground and left an offering by the tree, and then continued on carrying only my wand.

Suddenly the scene darkened and a huge presence loomed over from the clifftop. A huge, powerful and terrifying spirit of the land. A hundred feet tall, dark and djinn-like. He was the spirit of the moors and he demanded to meet with me.

I opened my eyes with a start and found myself back in the clearing. I did not know what the earth spirit wanted but I didn't feel like the time was right for me to confront such a powerful being!

I looked around and the place now seemed more magical than ever. It was vibrant and buzzing with energy. Ivy climbed and cascaded over the rocks all around me. I continued on, heading further westward along the steep wooded slope until I came up against a dark rock face.

I was met by a sinister-looking dark elf commander wearing black armour and an intricate, tight-fitting black helmet. Was this the same dark elf I had met on Hood Hill? He seemed to have a similar energy about him. I didn't trust him though and was slightly afraid of him.

But I did trust my intuition... suddenly it became clear to me what I must do! I was afraid of the consequences and performed the act in a kind of daze, but I found myself drawing my sword of light, the otherworldly weapon I had retrieved from Dunino. The dark elf looked at me with a challenge in his eyes but before he had chance to say anything I struck him down with my sword of light!

I felt a surge of energy as the light overcame the darkness! A sudden shift to a higher state of being and a heightened awareness. I am the bringer of light! I am Aurvandil the luminous wanderer! I felt myself grow and it was as if I had a huge pair of wings like an angel. I was filled with white light, and the light from my wand and my sword burned with a blinding brightness! Darkness had been banished by the light!

Feeling elated I opened my eyes and the evening sun was shining brightly into the clearing where I was standing. I walked towards a gap in the trees and soaked up the intensity of the sun's rays, absorbing its light and then casting it out in all directions like I was a star myself. What an overwhelming experience it had been!

I climbed to the base of the cliff and rested my back against it. As I sat down I tuned in to the energies of this secluded place.

I sensed a presence in the trees and then noticed a face peering out from behind one of them. It was a faery maiden, blonde and beautiful, giggling to herself as she looked at me. Was this the same faery maiden I had seen in Lindsaylands? She certainly seemed very familiar to me. She ran from tree to tree, laughing to herself and peering out at me. She seemed more carefree and abandoned than any human woman could ever be.

Suddenly I remembered her... I had always known her! Overwhelmed with delight I rose up to greet her, but she was gone...

It was now getting late and would soon be dark, so I made my way back along the base of the cliff, back out through the forked tree and back into the mundane world. The Devil's Parlour would have to wait until the next day.

* * *

The following morning I decided to take a different approach. I walked through a wooded valley to the northeast of Roulston Scar that is known as Happy Valley, and made my way to a small footpath that led up to the top of the cliffs. I followed the footpath until I could see the cliffs looming to my left and then headed off through the undergrowth towards the base of the cliffs where they met with the top of the steep wooded slope.

I then followed the base of the cliffs, scrambling up and down, climbing over trees and rocks. Progress was slow, but I checked every nook and cranny in the cliff face and I knew that if there were a cave here then I was eventually going to find it! A few promising looking holes and fissures led nowhere, but as I rounded a corner in the cliff I came to a fissure larger than any I had seen previously and I knew that this had to be it!

I climbed up to the entrance and squeezed inside, it was not a large cave by any means and the narrow crevice only led a few yards into the cliff, but it was a cave! And a cave with enough of a reputation to at some point have been given the name of the Devil's Parlour. But why? Perhaps that was what I was here to find out.

I crawled deep inside the crevice and once I reached the end I sat down and meditated.

I called upon any spirits here to show themselves. After a while I sensed the presence of a small humanlike creature. It was a hob, a hobgoblin like the one I had met at Hob Holes. He hid deep within the dark recesses of the cave and didn't want to come out.

I asked him why he was afraid and he told me that a priest had cast a spell upon him and banished him to the darkness, he couldn't leave his cave any longer and was trapped in this dark otherworld. I promised him that I could break the spell, that he no longer had any need to be afraid, that the Christian priests did not hold power here any longer. Then I took him by the hand and led him out into the light...

Cautiously he exited the cave and suddenly he beamed with elation! He told me how, long ago, the druids used to come to his cave regularly to seek his aid. Druids and locals alike would leave offerings of food there for him; but then the Christians came and called him a devil! They forbade the local people to visit him anymore and they cast wards and spells and banished the poor hob.

But now he was free again! He jumped and leaped for joy, and then tumbled head over heels down the hillside and disappeared into the trees below.

“Well now I know why it's called the Devil's Parlour”, I thought! No doubt a similar cave nearby called the Fairies' Parlour also had such a story attached to it.

I decided to continue a little further around the base of the cliff and made some curious finds. Firstly the imprint of a fossil ammonite. Then a small rock shelter filled with feathers and snail shells. And finally a mummified rat, which I decided to leave behind for future explorers to discover!

Roulston Scar may have many more mysteries still to be uncovered...

Claymore Well and Wade's Stone

28th January

I was intrigued by a story from Kettleness, North Yorkshire, of a spring known in folklore as Claymore Well where it was said that the sound of the fairies could be heard at night "beating their bittles and battledores". Research on the internet indicated that the well could no longer be found but I decided to visit the area anyway to investigate some of the nearby springs and pools, and also the mysterious Wade's stone which sits nearby. It has associations with a mythical giant called Wade, and has stories of strange supernatural phenomena.

I drove over the moors and parked in Goldsborough Lane just south of the small village of Goldsborough and was drawn to a spot on the map where five trackways seemed to meet. Perhaps this was an important crossroads in times gone by? I set off on foot down the edge of a cultivated field and the first thing I spotted was a couple of hares grazing on one of the grassy verges near the far hedge, they were the first of many wild hares that I spotted that day.

I continued on towards the crossroads and dropped down over an odd-looking field boundary, like a low drystone wall that had been set into the ground, causing the field I had just crossed to appear like it was on a raised platform. I followed this boundary wall all the way to the crossroads but could not work out its significance, it seemed mysterious somehow, and very ancient.

I passed straight over the crossroads and came to a large grove of alder trees on my right that were marked on the map as Stangoe Carr. The ancient, twisted, stunted trees looked somehow mystical and drew me to investigate them further. I knew that on the far side of the carr stood Wade's stone so perhaps I could make a shortcut somehow? I should have known better though, a carr is basically a swamp full of trees and this one was no exception, the ground was completely flooded!

Searching around, I did manage to find a narrow raised causeway heading into the centre of the swamp, so I decided to follow it. Perhaps the causeway had once been traversed by people in times gone by, but now it was completely overgrown, with mature trees growing right through it. I had to climb under branches and over roots, startling many ducks in the process, who clearly were not used to clumsy humans crashing through the undergrowth!

Eventually I came to a point where the causeway sank down into the swamp and nothing lay ahead except open water dotted with trees. I stopped there and stood in silence for a while, and became aware of the intense sound of dozens of small birds chirruping all around me that I had not noticed while forcing my way down the causeway. The winter sun beamed brightly through the bare branches of the trees adding a magical aspect to this wild place. I took a closer look at the swamp and at some of the birds which darted from branch to twig all around me. I noticed that they were pretty, bright-yellow little birds called siskins, so I took out my camera and tried to get a shot of some of them.

But as I did so a very strange thing happened... I heard a sudden whooshing sound all around me! Directly over my head, to my right and to my left, all at the same time, seeming to come from both near and far.

"Whoosh! Whoosh-whoosh!"

It sounded like the wings of a glider, or a kite straining in a high wind, or a flock of geese flying past at high speed, except that the sound seemed to come from all directions at once! It went on for several seconds and then just as suddenly stopped. I was left feeling as though invisible beings with bat-like wings had just taken off whooshing into the air, disturbed from their secret tryst by my uninvited presence and intrusive camera. The invisible alien from the film "Predator" came to my mind, strange indeed!

But I was not afraid, I stood there in silence, half-hoping that the sounds would return, but all I could hear were the chirps of the siskins who were still hopping through the branches all around me, singing away as if nothing had happened. Undaunted I stood in silence a little while longer, before making my way back out of the mysterious marsh.

I could not penetrate the swamp and so instead I followed the edge of the wood, all along its south side and then the east side until I came to the northern edge of the wood where I could see Wade's stone in the distance, standing alone in a field. It is not a huge and impressive standing stone, but it did look ancient and weathered, deep channels on its surface telling of the passage of thousands of years of wind and rain as it sat there exposed to all the elements.

As I neared the stone I thought I heard the strange whooshing sounds coming from the trees again! Could this be the sounds of "bittles and battledores" mentioned in the folklore of this place? In the olden days they would wrap newly-washed damp linen around a large rolling pin and sweep across it with a bittle or battledoor in a backwards and forwards motion until the linen was dried and flattened. The bittle was like a long flat piece of wood with a handle, sometimes elaborately carved. Could this produce a similar whooshing sound if passed back and forth fast enough? It was something I would have to experiment with later.

I walked around the stone several times and then sat down with my back to it, but I didn't experience any of the strange phenomena that other visitors to the stone had sometimes reported, I just got a sense that somehow this stone was drawing energy down into the land.

I headed westward now towards Brockrigg Farm to go looking for the fabled Claymore Well. As I passed by Brockrigg Farm a strange pool to my left drew my attention, but I continued on towards Claymoor House to see if there was any sign of a well around there. There was no-one around to ask so I searched all around the building and the field boundaries but could find nothing, so I decided to return to the pool I had spotted near Brockrigg Farm.

The pool looked semi-natural and there was a spring there issuing forth water, so perhaps this was it! I sat down there, closed my eyes and tuned in.

I sensed a presence in the water, and then the hideous face of a hag emerged from the depths! She had sharp, pointed teeth, and hair of matted pond weeds. I tried to talk with her but she was not forthcoming, so I decided to leave before she turned nasty.

I walked back past Claymoor House towards the sea cliffs and then followed a trackway and field boundary to an old burial mound called Butter Howe. I was intrigued by the name as there were stories of 'fairy butter' from this area.

There was an ancient spirit living there in the mound, but he did not like to be disturbed and he didn't like people tramping all over him!

I assured him of my good intentions and then climbed the mound and planted my wand on the summit, drawing down energy into this sacred place.

I explored some more of the local landscape features and then returned to my car. What had I discovered today? The strange sounds of "bittles and battledores" that I now believed came from the swamp and not from the well. The sound was said to have been heard for "miles around", so did it necessarily have to come from one particular spot? And was it the fairies making these sounds, or something more sinister? Weren't all strange supernatural beings at one time described as 'fairies' anyway? I truly believed that I'd had a close encounter out there in the swamp, but with what? Well whatever they were they did not reveal themselves to me at this time, so it would have to remain a mystery.

Mulgrave Woods and Jeanie the Fairy

29th January

As I was already in the area I felt like the time was now right to visit Mulgrave Woods. I remembered what the dark elf had told me about placing a crystal there, and whether I trusted him or not I still felt like I had to investigate.

Folklore tells that Mulgrave Woods in North Yorkshire were the abode of Jeanie the Fairy. She was said to live there in a cave called Hob's Cave and to dislike visitors intensely. She would cast curses on anyone who bothered her and many a local misfortune was blamed upon the malevolence of this mysterious spirit. Long ago a brave and foolish local farmer who had probably had a bit too much to drink, decided to go and find this elusive fairy for himself, to purge the place of her misfortune once and for all. But as soon as he laid eyes upon her terrible form, his courage failed him and he leapt back on his horse and fled in terror. Jeanie chased him and he only escaped with his life when he remembered that the spirit could not cross running water, so he galloped for the nearest stream and leapt across it. As he did so Jeanie struck the horse with her wand and cut it in two! The farmer just managed to reach the safety of the other side before his horse fell down dead.

> "A very mischievous fairy, Jeanie of Biggersdale, resided at a place so called at the head of Mulgrave Woods. A bold young farmer, perhaps under the influence of John Barleycorn, undertook one night, on a wager, to approach the habitation of this sprite, and to call her : but his rashness nearly cost him his life; Jeanie angrily replied that she was coming, and while he was escaping across the running stream he fared worse than Burns's Tam O'Shanter, when pursued by Nanny the witch; for Jeanie overtaking him just as his horse was half across, cut it in two parts though fortunately he was on the half that got beyond the stream !"

This snippet of folklore was all I had to go on, so I took out a map and located Mulgrave Woods. I was surprised to discover that the woods were still completely intact and covered an extensive area on a private estate, filling a whole valley which contained two streams with many side valleys and gullies. The woodland extended almost all the way to the sea at Sandsend and reached inland for several miles, its many branches following stream beds and gullies deep into the countryside. Exploring this huge area was going to be a daunting task!

Further investigation pointed me towards one of the side gullies with a high waterfall, famously known as Biggersdale Hole. Could this be it? The steep gully leading down into the hole was called the Wizard's Glen and was reputed to be a magical place. I was intrigued and so I decided to investigate...

I set off in the morning, crossing the North York Moors until I reached the seaside town of Sandsend, just north of Whitby. The sky was cloudy and pregnant with rain so I didn't fancy a long hike through the woods and instead opted to drive around the woodland to a farm located just above Biggersdale Hole. I parked my 4x4 vehicle in a field and soon found the stream that led me directly to the waterfall. The small trickling stream suddenly transformed into a torrent of water as it disappeared over a lip of rock and plunged into a hidden gorge deep below.

I gingerly crept around the edge of the gorge on tiny rabbit trails but could find no possible way down the sheer sides.

I sat there and meditated, I could sense an entrance at the base of the waterfall, a hidden doorway to the otherworld, somehow I had to get down there!

I was left with no option but to follow the top of the gorge and hope that the sides became less steep further downstream. I was able to walk through the field that adjoined the gully, but unfortunately the sides of the gully were sheer for its entire length and it was only when I reached the main valley directly ahead that I was able to scramble down and eventually made my way down to one of the bigger streams in the valley, which was called East Row Beck.

Now all I had to do was follow the bank of East Row Beck until I came to the small stream that flowed out of Biggersdale Hole! The going was tough and sometimes I had to leave the flooded riverside and climb up the steep banks into the forest again, but eventually I made it to the entrance of the steep-sided valley. There was a clearing there with a little wooden footbridge crossing the steam, now all overgrown and little used. The hint of a pathway, long overgrown, also led into the Wizard's Glen.

The day was overcast and misty now and so the glen seemed incredibly magical and mysterious. It may have been a trick of the light but as I stood there I kept catching movements out of the corner of my eye, as if hidden spirits were darting from tree to tree, watching me. Apart from the bubbling of the stream, dampened by the mist, the silence was total, and I was completely alone there, but the place was so magical that it lifted my spirits and drew me onwards into the glen. The old pathway soon came to an end, petering out by the tiny stream and disappearing into undergrowth and fallen branches. The magical feeling was now giving way to a more sinister one, so I decided I'd better tune in and ask permission to continue first. I was told to drop an offering of food into the stream, and also to place my new batch of fluorite crystal eggs in there too (I had recently purchased these). I did as instructed and the food floated off downstream, while the eggs glittered under the surface of the water.

The eggs would be infused with energy, I was told, but I must leave them there.

I now felt like I had been given permission to enter and so I pushed on through the bushes, waded through the stream and climbed over fallen branches. The going got tougher and tougher the further I continued. Clearly no-one had been this way for a long time! I could sense the presence of Merlin above me, he seemed to be encouraging me to continue. Was this his glen? The Wizard's Glen?

Ahead of me whole trees had fallen down the gully into the stream, it seemed impossible to go on. I wanted to turn back, to get out of this forbidding place, but the silent encouragement of Merlin willed me forward. I climbed over the fallen trees, through thorn bushes and over wet slippery rocks and after an exhausting struggle finally I neared the end of the gully and could hear the tumbling waterfall ahead!

The head of the gully was rocky and barren, and the rocks slick with spray from the waterfall. It didn't look so deep as it had done from above, but still there was no way out other than the way I had come in. Carefully I climbed over the wet rocks and sat down by the pool in front of the waterfall and got my breath back.

As I tuned in there I projected my spirit through the waterfall and through the wall of rock behind, and suddenly found myself standing on a green hillside. There I was met by a young troll with shaggy black hair. He seemed happy to have company and he danced and played with me, and eventually we tumbled off down the hillside, head over heels, until we stopped by the side of a bubbling stream. We sat there and talked like old friends. I asked him if the Wizard's Glen was Merlin's Glen. He told me it was not, but that Merlin was always with me when I needed to call on him. He also told me that I would not find Jeanie the Fairy here, I needed to look elsewhere in the woods.

I returned to the rocks by the waterfall. It seemed like all my efforts had been in vain, but I was not despondent and was happy to have found such a magical place. As I looked down I then saw a red stone gleaming in the water, so I reached for it and picked it up.

Merlin spoke to me and informed me that this stone would add fire to my wand.

I wasn't quite sure what he meant by that but I popped the stone in my pocket before starting on the arduous hike back out of the gully.

I felt a lot more relaxed now and the sense of foreboding had completely gone. Only now could I truly appreciate the beauty of the place. As I walked slowly back, taking in the atmosphere, I suddenly noticed a white feather falling from the sky directly in front of me. I reached down and picked it up and then looking to my left noticed a row of small holes like rabbit holes that seemed to have been carved directly into the conglomerate rock that made up the sides of the gorge. I couldn't see how they could have formed naturally and the rock looked too hard to have been carved out by animals.

I sat down there and tuned in and soon realised that a colony of small boggles dwelt there, living halfway between our world and the otherworld, the shallow holes being entrances to their subterranean realm. Slowly they crept out and as I had done in other places I planted my wand into the ground there and sent them healing. The boggles were happy here in the Wizard's Glen, they felt secure and protected by the isolation and needed no help from me, but they were not aware of the other communities of boggles that I had encountered. They could not leave the area of the glen and the nearby forest and so had never ventured out into the wider world. I told them that this would soon change, and that sometime in the future they would be free to roam the world again.

After more scrambling and climbing I finally made it back to the walking trail where my fluorite eggs still lay glistening in the water. I picked them up and they seemed to feel fresh and energised. Holding them up to the light all the flaws and fractures in the crystals seemed to shimmer as if they had been coated in a thin layer of gold leaf. I was sure they had looked nothing like this before! They were now ready for whatever purpose my guides had in store for them.

I now found a small path leading up the side of the gorge that I had not noticed before. The path was quite broad but was overgrown. Clearly it had once been constructed by human hands for some unknown purpose. I decided to follow it as I thought it might provide a shortcut back to my car. As I neared the top I took one last look back into the Wizard's Glen, half-expecting to see faery forms dancing through the air, but the glen was silent.

I pushed on through the rhododendrons and was startled to encounter what I at first thought to be a small holy well constructed of natural blocks of stone, but on closer inspection appeared to be some kind of small shrine. A shrine to the fairies maybe? Out here in the middle of the forest?

I left a small offering there and continued on. Following the path to a knoll just above the shrine I then found an old abandoned summer house hidden in the undergrowth. Was this the answer to the mystery? In times gone by the landowner must have built this summerhouse, and the shrine, with the path leading up to it from the valley. Some Victorian romantic folly perhaps?

Then I made the strangest discovery of all, a dead cock pheasant lying suspended in a tree as if he had just recently tumbled down out of the sky. I inspected the pheasant closer and I could reach no other conclusion than that was what had actually happened. How strange! This was not the first nor the last time that I was to encounter dead birds that had seemingly fallen from the sky, but what was the meaning of it?

I continued down the path and was happy to find that I was soon heading back in the direction of my car, it had been an amazing detour, full of discoveries, but I was still no closer to finding Jeanie the Fairy. I referred to the folklore once more: "a place so called at the head of Mulgrave Woods." Perhaps I needed to try higher up the valley?

I checked the map and saw that there was an old motte (a castle mound) hidden in the woods near the head of the valley, it was called Fosse Castle, and I remembered that it had some old folklore associated with it and was said to be built by a giant. The old motte was abandoned in the thirteenth century when a newer medieval castle was built right in the centre of the valley.

I took a long drive around to the other side of the valley and parked near High Lees Farm. I then followed a very wet, boggy footpath back down into the valley until I came upon a tree-covered mound near the valley bottom, the old motte of Fosse Castle! I stepped up onto the flat-topped motte and paced around its upper rim wondering how I was going to find the home of Jeanie the Fairy, which in one tale is known as Hob's Cave. Beneath me the valley tumbled down into a rocky gorge where a stream cascaded over a jumble of dark and damp looking rocks. Any number of dark shadows under the rocks could have been the entrance to a cave, but how was I to explore such difficult terrain?

I decided to scramble into the gorge in any case, just to see what I could find, and was relieved to discover an old partly-overgrown path down near the bottom. Turning right I followed the path upstream towards the head of the gorge, but the path petered out and I soon found myself scrambling over rocks and climbing up the side of small cascades. The rocks were slippery and at one point my foot slipped into a pool, soaking it.

Eventually I came to a point where I could go no further, the rocks were just too slippery and steep, but the place looked absolutely magical! Bright green moss coated all the rocks and a huge hollowed-out basin lay to the left that must have been carved out by swirling rocks over many thousands of years.

Gazing through the undergrowth I was startled to discover that to my right were the remains of an old building. So weathered and overgrown with ivy that at first glance it looked just like a part of the rock face.

I sat down there in this enchanted spot by the stream and cast a quartz crystal into the water. I called upon Jeanie to show herself to me if indeed she dwelt here.

I waited a short while, tuning in to the energies of the place, and then I saw a woman appear! A strikingly attractive, powerful woman with flame-red hair that seemed to sweep up into the air like it was actually composed of flames. She did not appreciate being disturbed but when I explained to her my purpose she assented and agreed to show me the way to her cave dwelling. She took me by the hand and floated off to the north east.

I awoke and tried to follow her physically but I could not keep up with her, and my way was blocked by the steep sides of the gully. I tried several times to scramble up but each time was defeated.

By now it was starting to get dark, so with regret I had to abandon my quest for that day.

I later picked up an old Victorian novel called "Jeanie o' Biggerdale" which was set in a mill house by the stream in Mulgrave Woods. I realised with a start that the old building I had discovered was indeed the mill house mentioned in the book! And the gully that I had been sitting in was where the woman in the tale had committed suicide by casting herself down onto the rocks because she was unable to be with her true love. The whole tragedy was caused by the curse of Jeanie the Fairy. After reading about the genteel lifestyle of those dwelling in the manor house and how they would take walks in the grounds of the forest it also explained to me the magical paths I had discovered and the old summerhouse. How mysterious it felt that the place was now so abandoned and reverting back to its more ancient and natural state. Perhaps Jeanie still jealously guarded her realm and put paid to any plans to develop the place by casting one of her renowned and much feared curses!

Mulgrave Woods was clearly still an important spot for anchoring the mysterious energies of the North York Moors. I had left a crystal there as instructed by the dark elf on Hood Hill, balancing the energy of the crystal placed on the other side of the moors. Now I just had to find "the centre of the grid," wherever that was!

Obtrush Roque, The Hobgoblin's Cairn

3rd February

Long ago a farmer in Farndale on the North York Moors was being much disturbed by a malicious hobgoblin or hobman. Not able to bear the malicious pranks of the hobman anymore the farmer eventually decided to quit his farm. He packed all his belongings into a cart and set off on his way, but before he got far one of his neighbours asked him where he was going.

"We're flitting!" the farmer said.

At which point the butter churn suddenly opened up and the hobman's head popped out.

"Aye, we're flitting!" said the hobman!

Realising the hopelessness of his situation the despondent farmer returned home to his farm.

This short tale has parallels in other parts of the country and in Scandinavian folklore too, but this particular hob, the Farndale hob, was associated with a mysterious mound of stones up on the moors called Obtrush Rook, or the Hobgoblin's Cairn, which is made up of the remains of an ancient mound of stones containing a burial cist.

Intrigued by the story I decided to try and visit this almost completely forgotten location and see what power, if any, the place still held. I drove to Farndale and parked in a narrow country lane by a nearby farm called Kneysbeck. The start of the climb followed a public footpath past an ancient spring that flowed into a stone trough. The path then continued up the hillside through some woods before emerging into an old overgrown country lane that ran along the back of the cultivated valley.

Here I left the public footpath and followed the old lane for a while before it too became little more than a track, heading up the hillside onto the high moors. The trackway passed through hidden gullies tucked away into the hillside and occasionally provided magnificent views over the valley of Farndale, now far below me.

Using my compass and various landmarks I determined where the path reached its nearest point to the fabled cairn and then set off on foot over the heather, leaving the trackway behind me. It did not take long struggling uphill before I could see the top of the ridge far ahead of me, and there, almost directly to my front, sat the cairn! There were some other piles of stones further over to the right, but I was sure from my calculations that I had the right place in my sights, and the closer I got the more certain I became, as this structure stood alone near the very summit of the ridge.

As I got closer the stones took on a rather more forbidding aspect, I did not feel invited or welcome, so I decided to start by walking around the stones sunwise. Not only could this be taken as a sign of respect but it also gave me chance to familiarise myself with the location. There seemed to be an outer circle of stones surrounding an inner pile, as well as one section on the outside that seemed to have been formed up into wall or shelter of some sort.

I noticed that many of the stones were cup-marked, but whether this was natural or carved by the ancient hand of man was hard to tell.

After processing around the stones three times I then stood by what seemed to be the entrance and asked permission to enter.

As I closed my eyes I could see a vision of the hobgoblin standing in the centre of the stone circle. He was larger than me and demonic-looking with an unfriendly aspect, and he did not want to be disturbed!

As a further sign of respect I placed a scallop shell by the entrance to the mound and filled it with honey.

This got him more interested. He realised now that I wasn't just some hiker come to disturb him, I was here for a purpose!

"What do you bring?" he rasped.

I produced a large quartz crystal from my bag. He told me to leave all else behind and enter with the crystal, so I dropped my bag and stepped forward.

I was apprehensive and didn't really trust him, but he let me walk right into the centre of the cairn. I stood on the mound of rocks in the centre and placed my crystal there, down amongst the rocks.

As soon as I did so a huge and powerful column of white light shot down from the sky! It filled the cairn with its energy and caused the whole cairn to glow with light, which slowly issued forth from the cairn in all directions down snakelike pathways out across the moors. I was filled with this light and energy and could see the glowing pathways all around, slithering away like white-hot molten serpents in all directions, being carried far out across the land.

In my mind's eye I followed these trails and saw them emerging as a stream of sparkling stars in bubbling springs. Springs all over the moors were filled with this energy! The energy poured forth from the edges of the moors into the rivers to be carried by them across the plains. Lake Gormire too I saw sparkling with this new energy. The springs had been energised! A new magic was issuing from them to be carried far out across the land. I had found the centre of the grid!

Finally the column of light subsided but now I too was transformed. I stood there as Aurvandil, the luminous wanderer, in white silken clothing with a blue crystal pendant and silken hair of yellow gold. A powerful faery woman appeared before me in a long flowing green dress with flowing hair of reddish blonde. It was Queen Maeve my faery guide! She told me that I had done well and that the first stage of my quest was now complete. I was told that I was on my way to receiving a great prize, and then she stroked my face seductively.

I opened my eyes and the vision was gone. My work was done here.

I returned to the bottom of the hill and passed by the spring again. It was filled with a magical energy, but I noticed now that the water in the spring was no longer flowing. Odd, I thought.

Back at my car I took out a pair of newly acquired dowsing rods and thought that I would give them a go as I had never tried dowsing before. They were heavy L shaped rods made of copper. I walked back up to the woods and found a suitable clearing and stood there with the rods pointing directly forward.

The results astonished me! Whenever I asked for a positive response the rods crossed over strongly into an X shape as if guided by unseen hands. The nearest thing I can equate it to is a Ouija board where the glass seems to move by itself. I then tried dowsing for underground water and almost immediately found a vein of water, and then when I found an underground spring the rods crossed over violently.

"Was that the wind!" I said to myself.

The rods immediately swung outwards in a violent negative response! OK, now I was convinced... This was the nearest thing to real magic I had ever experienced in the physical world!

I asked the rods if there was anything else to discover here, but the rods fell silent.

I later realised that the location I had discovered, the hobgoblin's cairn, was the omphalos, the very spiritual centre, or navel, of the North York Moors. By energising its centre I had effectively energised the whole of the moors and carried that energy outwards and beyond, into all the land around.

Aberfoyle, Doon Hill and the Fairies

6th February

My next trip was to one of the most well known and magical fairy locations in the British Isles. Doon Hill in Aberfoyle, Scotland is where the Reverend Robert Kirk had many encounters with the Fae back in the seventeenth century. He wrote a book about his experiences entitled "The Secret Commonwealth of Elves, Fauns and Fairies" which is now famous amongst fairy folklorists. But his obsession was to be his undoing, because one day he was abducted by the fairies and was never seen again. People say that there is an entrance to the Otherworld on Doon Hill through which the reverend passed, and some say that he dwells up there still, in the Land of the Fae.

Doon Hill lies just south of Aberfoyle on the far side of the River Forth in an area of extensive woodland. The hill itself is shrouded in forest giving it a mysterious appearance.

I walked down the lane from Kirkton and approached the hill from the west. As soon as I entered the trees at the base of the hill there was a magical atmosphere that pervaded the woodland all around me. The trees looked spindly and twisted, and dewy moss shone bright and green on the boughs. Strange rock formations were scattered all around, covered in gnarly trees, they each looked like miniature fairy mounds. I spotted a forked tree on top of one these small mounds which looked invitingly like an entrance to the fairy realm, so I climbed up and stepped through it, dropping down into a magical land on the other side.

I had stepped through a portal and from this point forth the edge between reality and fantasy became blurred so that all the events that I am about to relate to you happened in a kind of half trance.

I passed through the open woodland towards the summit of the hill, visible ahead of me, standing tall and proud like a fortress.

I could sense figures up there like soldiers standing on battlements and then I could see multi-coloured banners flying, I was surely approaching a fairy fort! I stopped and stared cautiously, and then I saw a couple of the elven soldiers descending from the fort to greet me, but they didn't look particularly friendly. They wanted me to relinquish all my weapons and amulets and then accompany them unarmed into the fortress, but fearing a trap I declined and so they withdrew.

Summoning all my energy and will power I then stepped forward but immediately I sensed missiles like arrows being fired at me. They struck me like bolts of light energy but seemed to bounce off harmlessly. Perhaps I was protected? I asked to be allowed entrance to the fortress but again they refused and launched more missiles, so I decided to back off under the onslaught and try a different approach.

I retreated out of range and left an offering of honey by a tree, and then covered myself in the pleasant scent of lavender oil to make myself more agreeable to the fairy folk. I headed northward, skirting around the western edge of the fortress and unexpectedly came upon another path! Instinctively I knew that I was now on the correct path to approach the fortress, the path just seemed more natural and had a gentler approach. Clearly I had been trying to enter the wrong way before! I followed this path until I stood at the foot of the fortress on the northern side.

I then gazed up at the battlements and this time a beautiful elf-maiden came down to greet me. She took me by the hand and led me happily and eagerly up the slope, almost giggling to herself.

At the top of the hill lay a magical clearing where people had left all kinds of offerings both around and in the trees there. Everything from clootie rags to crystals to fairy statues to wind chimes, the clearing was full of the stuff! At the centre of the woodland clearing stood a lone tree, on the very spot where the reverend Robert Kirk had disappeared into fairyland, never to be seen again!

I was guided by the elf maiden directly to this tree and I knelt down before it.

Beneath the roots of the tree was a small hole like the entrance to an animal burrow that led deep underground, and beside this hole several offerings had been placed including, candles, statues and ribbons. I found a green glass half filled with rainwater and dirt and decided to clean it out and leave another offering of honey there for the fairies.

The maiden took me by the hand again and this time led me straight down into the hole. Now I felt like I really was entering the Otherworld! We went down and down and down through the darkness and then suddenly emerged onto a grassy meadow by an old-fashioned farmhouse. The sun was shining and the elf maiden was still holding my hand, except she was no longer an elf maiden she was a little girl, and I was a little boy! She giggled playfully and memories came rolling back to me. I was in a past life! The little girl was my true love, we grew up together all our lives from being little children. I never knew this before, but it explained so much! It explained why she had meant so much to me and why her eventual loss was so unbearable, even after many lifetimes. She was my soulmate, happy, playful, mischievous but completely without malice, she meant everything to me.

The scene passed and I was back with the elf maiden again, and now the tears were filling my eyes.

"Show me more," I said to her.

She led me once more down through the roots of the tree, this time down a pink spiral staircase like the inside of a giant conch shell, through pink-walled chambers and past a gruff ogre-like guard. We then emerged into a paradise world of lush greenery that was full of tame animals going about their daily business. Or at least they seemed tame because they were totally unafraid of us. The elf maiden and I had shrunk to a small size and were now flying through this world on butterfly wings. We flew through clouds of other multi-coloured butterflies, over the tree tops and then across vast plains teeming with wildlife. I had surely now entered the

Otherworld realm of the Fae! A completely unspoilt land of beauty, perfection and unceasing natural harmony.

Ahead I could now see a castle, a fairy castle standing alone in the plain. We were heading directly towards it but for some reason I started to get fearful. I could sense dungeons within, darkness, dampness and solitude. I feared a trap, of being stuck in faeryland with no means of escape like Robert Kirk. I refused to continue and the elf maiden grew angry with me, she became ugly and hissed at me!

Suddenly I was back in my body! Back in the clearing on top of Doon Hill. What was the meaning of that castle? Was it revealing my inner fears or was it another scene from a past life?

I was standing facing the tree again with its mysterious entrance to the Otherworld, but when I turned around to face the clearing I had another vision.

I saw standing there a gathering of noble elf lords in long silvery silken robes. Their long straight silken hair hung down past their shoulders and they wore silver circlets upon their brows. They stood in a semi-circle around me and stared in my direction with arms hanging down by their sides, fingers interlocked before them, looking rather solemn.

"What have you brought us?" one of them said.

I remembered the green fluorite eggs in my bag, so I took them out and started to lay them out on the ground before me in the formation of a twelve pointed star.

"Too small!" said the elf lord.

I instinctively knew what he meant. The star should cover the entire clearing, with the otherworld tree at the centre. I looked around the clearing and could see that six trees formed a circle around it. These would be the six points of the outer star, and I would place the other six crystals between these and slightly nearer the central tree to form the inner star.

So I walked around the clearing planting a crystal egg just before the foot of each of the six trees. Curiously these six trees all had offerings placed around them too and ribbons tied to them, just as much as the central tree had. I then placed the six inner crystals at a point midway between each of the outer crystals and returned to the central tree to see what would happen.

The elf lords stepped forward, one of them standing over each of the crystals. There were twelve elf lords in total! I took out my wand and stood with one hand touching the central tree while my other hand held the wand aloft. I called in white light from the sky, that limitless source of power and energy. The white light collected in the crystal at the tip of my wand and passed through me into the tree. It then spread out underground as if following tree roots and emerged beneath each of the elf lords.

The elf lords started to glow a pale luminescent green which slowly increased in intensity becoming brighter and brighter until they were engulfed in bright glowing columns of intense green light. These columns then transformed into trees and at their tops they grew branches which started to spread out over the roof of the clearing, while underground the roots of the trees also grew outwards, interconnecting with each other until the twelve trees were linked into one living network. This network spread ever outwards until it covered the entire land in a dense canopy of trees, a single, breathing, interconnected web. It was like a vision of the future, or of the deep past, the land as it once was, and will one day be again, an endless forest, a true wilderness, a land fit for the Fae to dwell in once more!

The vision slowly faded and I took a walk around the clearing but was soon disturbed by visitors, this time of the more mundane human kind! We exchanged a few stories and the guy told me that I should visit a famous Neolithic ritual landscape called Kilmartin. I hung around until they left and then decided that I should do the fairies a favour by clearing up some of the rubbish that had been left around and some of the less appealing items of junk that had been tied to the trees. I stuffed a whole carrier bag full of rubbish and just as I was about to give up for the day I turned around and there dangling right in front of my eyes was a blue teardrop-shaped crystal!

It was exactly like the one I had seen myself wearing in the vision I had on Lindsaylands Fairy Mound, the very first time I had seen myself as Aurvandil! The Fae had told me then that I should find myself one exactly like it and I had spent a whole day searching through one of the largest gemstone warehouses in the country but could find nothing to match it. Yet here it was, on Doon Hill, dangling right before my eyes! I knew instantly that this was a gift from the Fae and that I was meant to take it. So I picked it up and pocketed it gratefully, giving thanks to the Fae for their gift.

Now I had surely done everything that I had come here for, so I decided it was time to head back down the hill. Before I lost sight of the clearing I stopped and turned around for one last look. The place looked magical in the late afternoon light. The outer trees seemed to glow with a green luminous light while the central tree stood there pale and grey. Movements flickered on the edge of my vision, I was sure that the Fae were hiding there in trees all around, watching me.

The Hobgoblin of Hobthrush Hall

13th February

Yorkshire folklore tells of a cave in the scarrs (cliffs) above Over Silton on the edge of the North York Moors called Hobthrush Hall which was said to be the home of a local Hobgoblin. I checked the small scale Ordnance Survey maps around Over Silton but could find no indication of a cave, so all I had to go on was the following piece of local folklore:

> "Over Silton. In the precipitous cliffs, a short distance north-west of the village, called 'the Scarrs,' is a cave in the rock, known by the name of Hobthrush Hall, which was formerly the abode of a goblin of somewhat remarkable character, who appears by the stories yet current relating to him, to have been possessed of great agility, as he was in the habit of jumping from the hills above his dwelling to the top of Carlhow Hill,

about half a mile distant. He was not of the malignant kind... On the contrary, he was one of those friendly to man... The Silton goblin was a true and faithful servant to a person named Weighall, who kept the village inn, and rented the land on which his hall was situate. It was Hob's invariable practice to churn the cream during the night, which was prepared for him the evening before, for which his reward was a large slice of bread and butter, always placed ready for him when the family retired to bed, and always gone in the morning. One night, the cream was put into the churn as usual, but no bread and butter placed beside it. Hob was so disgusted with this piece of base ingratitude, that he never came to churn more, and appears to have entirely left the neighbourhood. His dwelling yet remains, a rugged cave among the rocks, dark, wet, and uncomfortable, but extending a considerable distance underground."

Carlow Hill was just to the West of Over Silton and there appeared to be 'scarrs' or cliffs just to the north of the village, so that seemed like a good place to start looking.

Parking was difficult as the lanes around there were very narrow but I did manage to find a small layby just to the north of the village that was on the other side of some fields that sat above the scarrs. I didn't fancy climbing over the barbed-wire fences and upsetting the local farmers so I opted to skirt around the fields and enter the woods to the north of the scarrs.

I plunged into the trees, heading down a slope, and soon found myself at the base of the cliffs at their northern end. It was then just a matter of tracing the edge of the cliffs southwards until I came across a cave, simple! The cliffs stood at the top of a long steep slope but were clearly visible through the open woodland of spruce plantation.

I had no idea what the cave looked like though, how big it was, or even if it really existed! So imagine my elation after scrambling for ages through the undergrowth, when I eventually spotted two very obvious looking and inviting holes in the cliff face! I climbed up to them and saw old graffiti carved all around that must have been over a hundred years old, confirming that this must once have been a popular and significant place; a place once often visited, but now forgotten. I stepped through the small entrance and entered a much larger area inside. This was definitely the right place. Hobthrush Hall... home of the Hob!

I searched around the inside of the cave and followed a small passageway at the back which became smaller and smaller until only a hob could have fitted down it! Tantalisingly a tiny tunnel about a foot high seemed to lead deep into an underground realm but unfortunately I was too large to explore any further myself, so I left an offering there to the spirits and to the hob.

But I was not done yet, as I crouched in the tiny tunnel I noticed a cavity above my head which might just be large enough for me to squeeze my head and shoulders into if I stood upright. Slowly and gingerly I forced my head up into the tiny cavity, past spider's webs and cocoons until my head torch shone into the small cavity above. There were big shiny black spiders living in every crack and crevice in the rock, as well as other insects which were hibernating from the winter cold.

I did not fancy poking around in there so I dropped back down into the tunnel and returned to the main cave. I had been feeling rather drained for a few days so I decided not to do any spiritual investigations today, as the energies here seemed particularly heavy. I could feel a headache coming on and so I decided to content myself with the discoveries I had made so far.

I left the cave and continued onwards towards Over Silton through the woods. I hadn't gone more than a hundred yards when I found my way blocked by a fallen oak tree which I had to duck to pass under. For some reason I removed my woolly hat to do this and was astonished to see a large moth clinging to it! It was one of the largest and most beautiful moths I had ever seen, with a marbled pattern on its back and long feathery feelers sprouting from its head.

I stared at it for a while and then tried to make it fly off by giving it a gentle nudge, but the moth clung firmly to my hat. I nudged it a couple more times but it just would not budge. I was feeling tired but I knew then that he must have some kind of message for me.

"Ok, so what do you want?" I said with a sigh.

"Go back to Hobthrush Hall!" said the moth.

"No, I'm tired, I'll go back later," I replied.

"Now!" he said.

"Sorry I'm feeling too tired," I said.

The moth's feathery antennae twitched and they both pointed in the direction of the cave. This was a message I just couldn't ignore! Resigned to my duty I decided to climb back through the undergrowth to the cave. I tried to get the moth to leave my hat by transferring him to the branch of a tree, but he held on firmly. I had to just hold my hat in my hand and take the moth with me!

I re-entered the cave, placed my hat at the far end of the cave by the small tunnel, and then planted my wand in the centre of the floor to draw in energy there. I then sat down by the cave entrance to meditate. Soon after I sat down the moth flew up into the cavity and disappeared into the darkness! I took this as a sign to explore the cavity further which I'd been unwilling to do earlier.

I got up and returned to the small tunnel and noticed what looked like a hand print of white powder on the wall below the overhead cavity. I then climbed up and poked my head through the cavity, bolder this time and less afraid of all the spiders that lay hidden around I climbed up as high as I could and shone my torch into every little crevice.

This time I spotted curious formations in the rock, pieces of fossilised wood and strange 'egg stones' like the ones I had seen on Roulston Scar, except these ones still had their filling inside, a strange red clay-like material. I just could not imagine what these curious eggstones could be, they must be millions of years old!

My interest piqued I decided to explore more of the cracks and crevices in this cave to look for similar eggstones and indeed I did find more, just to the left of the cave entrance, while overhead I noticed what looked like a large fossilised beam of wood! Thoughts of ancient civilizations lost in mists of time came to mind, strange worlds millions of years old which today we can have no concept of.

I noticed that the end of this particular crevice was blocked by a couple of boulders, each almost a foot across. It almost seemed like they had been placed there deliberately and so I decided to remove them to see what lay behind. As I removed the last boulder I got quite a shock!

"Oh my God!" I said, because the boulders were hiding a tiny little doorway, perfectly rectangular and only a couple of inches high! At that moment I knew I had found it at last, everything had been guiding me to this very spot, the entrance to Hobthrush Hall!

The passageway was very narrow and even with my arm fully extended I could not reach the tiny doorway. As I shone my torch down and took photos of the doorway I felt a sudden rush of energy shoot out from it and I was overcome with dizziness! I fell back into the main cave and shook my head to prevent myself from passing out completely!

"I don't like all those lights!" shouted the hob from behind the tiny doorway.

"I'm sorry, I'll switch them off and I'll put the rocks back to hide your home again, I promise!"

I was nervous now, I had felt his power! So I replaced the rocks and left an offering of honey there for him.

"I thought you sent the moth to fetch me back?" I said.

"I did, but I don't like all those lights!" He was a grumpy little hob.

"Will others come?" he asked.

"Yes, but they'll treat you with respect, I promise!"

"Will they bring honey too?"

"Yes," I replied.

"Very well then," he said.

The hob was a powerful spirit. In the past he would have been treated with respect but nowadays so many of the hobs' haunts are overrun by tourists and so the hobs retreat underground, far from the eyes of mankind. This place was still relatively untouched and so the power of the hob was still strong. I hope that anyone who decides to visit this place will treat the hob with the respect he deserves and leave a small offering for him in the cave.

I picked up my things and left the cave, but then I remembered that I had left my hat lying in there. I popped back in to grab it off the floor and I heard the voice of the hob one last time.

"Thank you," he said simply.

The Fairy Cross Plain and Danby Heads

4th March

After acquiring more fluorite crystals and getting them energised at Lindsaylands fairy mound in Scotland it was time for me to return to the Fairy Cross Plain.

I knew I had an important task to complete today, so to avoid drawing attention to myself I did not start near the village as before but parked up on Danby Rigg and followed an old overgrown footpath down the side of the hill.

As I neared the edge of the rigg the views of the Fairy Cross Plain below were spectacular. The morning mist that hung in the valley was just about to clear and a large rolling curtain of cloud blotted out the sun but was just giving way to reveal a beautiful blue winter sky.

The rounded fairy hill that was the destination of my quest was clearly visible in the plain before me, sitting proudly like a huge green pimple. I scrambled on downwards through last-year's dried bracken and hopped over a drystone wall into the plain. The fairy hill beckoned before me but I looped around the back of the hill to avoid prying eyes, and then made my way past the rabbit holes that cluttered its flank until I reached the summit of the mound.

My first job was to retrieve the ten crystals that I had left there in January. I had popped them in the entrance to an old rabbit hole, but now, no matter how hard I tried I did not seem to be able to find them! Perhaps someone else had found them, or perhaps the rabbits had buried them deep underground? I had one last look and then finally I spotted them! I stuffed my hand in the hole and pulled them out, one, two, three... I managed to retrieve only seven in all, so now I had to stuff my arm right down the rabbit hole and root around, clawing out mud and turf until finally, with great relief, I retrieved the last one!

I placed them with the two new crystals I had brought along so now I had them all at last! Twelve fluorite eggs that had all been energised on the fairy mound at Lindsaylands in Scotland and had now been brought here to Yorkshire, for what purpose I did not know.

I sat there and meditated with the stones and the fairy king appeared, with white beard and cloak, looking much as he had the last time I had visited. He instructed me to lay them out in a twelve-pointed star and I remembered the pattern I had made at Doon Hill in Aberfoyle. What was the significance of this pattern?

I started to place the crystals all around the top of the hill, but the hill top was rounded and uneven, and the grass was long, so I soon started to lose track of where I had placed the crystals. I grew concerned and decided that I had to get all the crystals back before I forgot where they all were. I retrieved most of them but there was one which I just couldn't find no matter how hard I tried! I now had no idea at all where this crystal was, it could have been anywhere on the hilltop hidden in the long grass!

There was nothing for it, I took out my dowsing rods and decided that the only way I was going to find the crystal was to dowse for it. I walked around and around the hilltop with my rods out in front of me, focusing on the missing crystal. Suddenly the rods crossed over! I looked down at my feet and there it was, the missing crystal! If ever I needed proof that dowsing worked then surely this was it!

Happy to have my twelve crystals back again I walked to the very crown of the hill, stabbed my crystal tipped wand into the ground, and then laid out the crystals in a much smaller pattern around the wand. I now remembered that this was what I had attempted to do the first time I came here when I did not have enough crystals with me. I guess that my experience at Aberfoyle had distracted me into thinking that I had to lay the crystals out in a larger pattern. I had to learn never to assume that what's good for one place is suitable for another!

I stood there above my star grid, closed my eyes, and was just about to call in the energies when I heard the chugging of a tractor approaching the hill. It was the local farmer, no doubt come to give me a telling off for being on his land! I quickly grabbed up my wand and my dowsing rods and put them back in my bag, but by now he was upon me and he was not happy! Who knows how long he had been watching me and what he thought I was up to! He probably thought I was after his rabbits! I tried to explain to him that I was just here to dowse for energy lines but he did not want to know. Despite being only yards from a public footpath he basically harassed me until I was forced to leave.

No matter, I figured that I didn't have to be actually standing on the spot to call in the energies. I had left an imprint there and the crystals were still there in their star pattern, so all I had to do now was find a suitable spot to call down the white light to energise this place. I continued northeast, crossed the lane and climbed Danby Head opposite, which is a long hill that separates the two valleys of Great Fryupdale and Little Fryupdale.

When I reached the top of the slope I stood up there on Danby Crags and looked back down over the plain. The fairy hill was still clearly visible in the plain below me and so I took out my wand and started to focus. I pointed my crystal-tipped wand directly at the top of the mound and focused upon drawing energy down into the star pattern that I had created.

Immediately a huge column of blinding white light shot down from the sky and entered the crown of the knoll. The knoll then filled with energy, more and more of it, intensifying until the knoll seemed to glow from within. The top of the knoll then appeared to peel away to reveal a huge clear crystal like a column of pure shining quartz. The crystal filled with blinding white light until it could no longer contain the energy and then suddenly burst forth beams of white light in all directions. The beams connected this place to other similar places, filling them with energy and energising the grid.

So what did this vision mean? Was it a vision of the future, or was what I had witnessed actually happening right now, but on another level and in another dimension to the one we are consciously aware of in our day to day lives? I knew one thing though with certainty: the task that I had been given all those months ago by King Erowyn at Lindsaylands fairy mound was now complete. It felt strangely anti-climactic somehow, I knew I had achieved something, but what? And what next? "Fear of completion" is what Alphedia would have called it, or "being at a loose end" is how I would describe it!

I did some dowsing for guidance, asking Yes or No questions and getting answers from the rods. I was told to return to Scotland to meet the elves there, my job on the North York Moors was now completed.

Return to Scotland, Polveoch Burn, Aberfoyle and the Highlands

7th March

Having completed my quest for King Erowyn I returned to Lindsaylands fairy mound and met with my guide Atheron there.

The place seemed troubled, not so tranquil as it had done before, but eventually I was able to make contact with the king again.

As I stood on the mound meditating I saw myself as Aurvandil walking towards King Erowyn and his court and embracing the king's daughter. It was odd, I thought, usually I am Aurvandil but now I was seeing him in the third person. So is he me? Or is this a vision of another time, another world? He dwells in the land of faerie where all things are beautiful and timeless, yet here I am stuck in this human body with all my bodily cares and human woes. If I am to receive any reward for my efforts then perhaps these rewards are going to come to me in the Otherworld and not in this world? My task as a human being seems to be to release all my negative energies and fears, and raise myself to the level of the Fae so that I may join them again in their world. So have they tricked me again? Has it all been for nothing?

My human self was left pondering this as I turned to leave the fairy mound again, clearly there was nothing more for me to do here, my task for King Erowyn was done. I asked Atheron to accompany me and guide me, so that whenever I would lose my way I could call upon his help and guidance.

So I had been guided to return to Scotland to look for 'elves'? I realised that the word used was vague, that these were going to be different beings from the Fae that I had already encountered. I was guided to visit the Leadhills area of Lanarkshire and so I began my search there using my dowsing rods to guide me.

My guidance eventually led me to a remote windswept hillside known as Corbie Hall, I could not work out what a 'hall' was but it seemed to refer to some large underground chamber. I lay down in a small gully there to get out of the biting wind and tried to commune with the beings who lived there.

I could sense tall thin brown-skinned elfin spirits all around me. They had black bug-eyes and long pointed ears, their voices were rasping and unfriendly. They wouldn't talk directly to me but my guide Atheron was able to communicate with them.

"Two roads cross on high. Take the holy spear!" he translated.

I didn't know what it meant. Were these elves trapped here? Did they need this magic spear in order to free themselves? I was able to get that the cross was in Scotland (Ayrshire?) and that Hecate would show (or guard?) the way. I could sense other communities of elves around who were even less friendly, these were not the noble Fae I was used to.

* * *

I decided to leave Leadhills for now and head further west to Kirkconnel. I had heard an interesting piece of folklore about some fairy-haunted woods around there near the Polveoch Burn.

> "The braes of Polveoch, at the west end of the Bank Wood, was a favourite trysting place of the fairies. Here the good little folks assembled on May Day to celebrate the advent of summer; contingents came in from Kello Water, Glen Aylmer, and Glen Wharry, and when all had gathered together they rode merrily over the knowes towards the Bale Hill, in whose sun-ward slope a beauteous doorway was said to open for them, which they entered two at a time, the green turf closing over the last pair to get in. Hallowe'en was another of their gala nights.
>
> It is related that one Hallowe'en two farm servants, while on their way to Todholes to see their sweet-hearts, heard sounds of most enchanting music issuing from Polveoch Burn. Turning aside to discover from whence it came, they were astonished to see in a green opening among the trees a company of fairies, male and female, dancing to a band of pipers. All were dressed in the most elegant style, and their delicate little bodies swirled round in a fashion that quite entranced the awestruck swains. One, however, thought the strange sight could bode no good, and he beat a hasty retreat, leaving his companion gazing admiringly on the dazzling show. Long he stood and feasted his eyes and ears on the exquisite scene and the delicious melody, when, his presence being discovered by one of the company, he was invited to take part in the dance, and presented with fruit and wine. He daringly accepted; the refreshments seemed to put

a new life into him, and he joined in the dance with the most lively spirit, acquitting himself so well that he was made quite a hero by the little ladies in green, who did all in their power to make him enjoy himself. To drink of the fairies' wine was to lose all calculation of time, and twelve months went round and found the young fellow still enjoying himself with the wee folks. On Hallowe'en following he was found at the same place by his companion, who, refusing a drink that was proffered him, gave offence to the fairies, and, dragging hold of his friend, pulled him away, and broke the spell that bound him. He could scarcely believe he had been twelve months with the fairies, and said the time only seemed like an hour or two. Ever afterwards he was endowed with second sight."

I started by walking east through Bank Wood, a place which was once “much haunted” and still today is filled by ancient trees, protected between a steep slope and a modern railway line. I came across a beautiful spring under a rock ledge and as I meditated there I had a vision:

Small green glowing lights emerged from the hillside all around me, and I had a vision of the sidhe (trooping faeries), processing in their glowing white robes along the Polveoch Burn.

As I stood gazing at the spring I remembered the message I had got on the North York Moors. I was to place crystals in these springs in order to energise the waters, but unfortunately I had no crystals with me at this time.

I walked all the way along the base of Shiel Hill (Perhaps Shiel Hill derived its name from the sidhe?) and then climbed up to its summit. I stood there at the summit on a small square rock and had a vision of one of the sidhe riding up to me on a horse.

He was wearing a green robe and was quite confrontational, but I held him at bay with my wand and revealed to him my true form as Aurvandil. He then greeted me and he told me that I should return later in the year. Perhaps he meant on Beltane (May Day) when the fairy gathering takes place?

I also had a vision of the faerie king by the Polveoch Burn so I decided that it was time to go investigate this mysterious burn (stream) which ran past the far side of the hill. I walked downhill until I came to a small burn with a little waterfall. I followed it downstream and eventually came to a much larger waterfall that disappeared into a gully.

Unfortunately the water here seemed to be polluted with acid water draining from a mine, which somewhat spoilt the magic of the place, but it was a tranquil and beautiful spot nonetheless.

I followed the burn back to the road and further investigations in the area revealed nothing more that day. The elfin knight had told me to return later so maybe I had to visit the place on a date when the veils were thinner before this place would reveal more of its secrets to me?

* * *

My next stop was Aberfoyle where I intended to return to Doon Hill. I picked up my friend Tina and we headed off through the woods towards the famous fairy hill. I stepped through the forked tree that I had stepped through the first time I visited and as I did so a voice in my head said:

"Two times in, two times out!"

It was a reminder that the last time I came here I had forgotten to step back out the way I came in! Perhaps this was why I had been feeling so drained and spaced out since then? My head had been stuck in faeryland!

As we approached the fort I felt the bolts of energy being cast down at me again, but this time I did not resist and simply let them enter me. They seemed to be cleansing me and removing my negative energy! Why had I not trusted them the last time?

We reached the glade at the top of the hill where the magic trees with their hanging clootie rags stood and I was struck by the change in atmosphere there since the last time I had visited.. it was so much lighter and more airy and magical! The place looked clean and well cared-for and wind chimes gently tinkled giving it a serene atmosphere. It was almost as if the work I had done here the last time I came had raised the energy of the place and made it more light and magical.

Tina meditated and met with her spirit guides. She was then taken to see a bear and a beetle. The bear represented the strength in the land, but now that bears were extinct in the British Isles mankind had to find a way of fulfilling that role. The beetle said something very simple: "Remember the small things!"

The only message I got was to cleanse the blue teardrop-shaped pendant that I had discovered here previously, by placing it in a spring. After spending some time soaking up the magical atmosphere we headed back down the hill and this time I remembered to climb back through the forked tree, twice! So now I was back in the real world at last!

* * *

I said goodbye to Tina and continued my journey north, up into the wild Highlands of Scotland. I travelled up the eastern side of Loch Lomond. This is the less-visited and much wilder side of the famous loch and I headed as far north as the road would take me, to a tiny little place called Rowerdennan.

There I got out of my car and climbed up to a secluded little waterfall by a place called Rowchnock. I had come to this wild and secluded spot for a reason, to connect with the spirit of Mother Earth herself!

As I sat there meditating by the waterfall with the earth beneath me I suddenly experienced a huge surge of energy as I felt myself connecting with the spirit of the entire earth! I had never felt anything like this before! This was huge, powerful and terrifying!

As I felt this awesome power it made me realise how insignificant we all are, scratching a living here on the thin surface. The spirit of the Earth lives deep deep below and is all powerful! I wondered then if people in ancient times had felt this power as I was feeling it? If they held an awareness of this overwhelmingly powerful presence then it is no wonder that they treated the Earth with such reverence! Did they also feel the power of the sun and the moon in this way too? What an amazing thing is creation! How the powers of Earth, Sun and Moon keep everything in constant motion, ensuring that the Earth is constantly recreating itself. The winds blow, the clouds deposit their moisture, the rivers cut deep fissures in the earth, the continents shift, volcanoes create and destroy, and the atmosphere creates a perfect greenhouse that sustains all life.

All of this came to me in one moment, the awesome world that we live on. Everything of the earth is Gaia! One great living organism. Even all the creations of mankind are of Gaia. The clothes that we wear and the technology that we use, it all comes from Gaia and it will all go back to her as the Earth constantly recreates itself. We are nothing more than an itchy fungus on her skin, so insignificant and so small that Gaia is barely even aware of us!

But in that brief moment of communion with the Great Mother she was aware of me! She noticed me! I felt it!

I was playing with forces here more powerful than I could possibly comprehend! But what an exhilarating experience it was nonetheless!

* * *

I continued my journey further north until I arrived at Tyndrum where I wanted to search for a patch of ancient Caledonian pine forest by the name of Coille Coire Chuile that clung to a snowy mountainside.

My first attempt to reach the forest failed as the way was blocked by a deep and fast-flowing stream at the bottom of a gully.

But undeterred I tried another approach and walked from Tom na Croiche until I reached a rickety little footbridge that crossed the Allt Gleann Auchreoch stream. The 'bridge' was just a couple of railway lines with loose wooden sleepers in between that were all rotten and broken. Some of them had already disintegrated and fallen into the raging waters below, so I had to get down on my hands and knees and edge my way slowly across to avoid toppling into the stream!

I finally made it into the ancient pine forest and it was indeed a truly magical place, completely unlike any modern forestry plantation or managed woodland. The trees were widely spaced with twisting reddish boughs and a deep green canopy of pine needles.

I walked slowly through the ancient and silent forest, touching some of the trees as I went. The area seemed to be covered in mounds and dips and hidden gullies. I approached a wide basin-like depression in the centre of the forest that had a small mound in the middle of it, I spotted some roe deer ahead of me, idly grazing. I sat and watched them silently for a while before they eventually noticed me and skipped away. I then made my way to the small mound in the centre of the clearing and meditated there.

I got the sense of this tiny forest being like a fortress, holding out against the forces of change and the modern world, waiting patiently to repopulate the land once its time came again, once the unwelcome invaders had exhausted their energies and retreated. The modern world is unsustainable, and the trees silently waiting knew this.

But the trees here were not happy, the land was over-grazed and no young trees were growing. They were under siege and weakening. I drew energy down into the place, as much as I could, to help with their regeneration.

I continued on up the mountainside but the weather was starting to turn bad so I decided to head back and try to cross the stream higher up. I crossed a small stream and found myself on a high spit of land. I sat down there and plunged my wand into the earth where it sank deep into the peaty ground. I imparted more energy and healing into the land and then withdrew my wand to find it stained dark by the peat.

I tried to continue but found the larger stream ahead to be uncrossable, so eventually and with trepidation I had to make my way back to the rickety bridge with its rotting railway sleepers.

I had made my way up into the wilds of Scotland again and I'd had all kinds of interesting experiences and adventures, but now it was time to turn back for home and return to Yorkshire.

Tarn Hole Spring

22th March - Spring Equinox

After reading about some strange 'unknown structures' on the moors above Tarn Hole I decided that I would like to return there. The place was magical, a place of 'high energy', somewhere to immerse yourself in nature and recharge your batteries. The last time I had been there I had the experience of becoming the 'wild man of the woods.'

I walked back to the magical glade where I'd had these experiences previously and as I approached I saw a leaf suddenly dance up into the air and then settle back down to earth again. There was absolutely no wind so I took it as a sign that this place still wanted to show me its ancient magic. So I sat down there and meditated, and as I did so a small shiny greeny-blue fly landed on my knee and looked at me. It seemed like he had a message for me but I was in no hurry to go running off on another quest right now, so I just sat there soaking up the magical atmosphere of the place until the fly suddenly buzzed off, away across the stream.

After a while I got up and crossed the stream myself, and headed up the hillside through deep bracken that grew between small twisted oak trees. Soon enough I was out of the magical wooded valley and up on the high moorland, and it didn't take me long to find the stone structure that I had come here looking for.

It looked like an ancient shrine so I knelt before the small opening and left a food offering in there. I then got up and did some dowsing to try and see what I could find out about this place, and as I did so a large bumblebee suddenly appeared out of nowhere and buzzed round and around my head several times.

He said he was sent by Marielle, the spirit of this place, and his message to me was that I should sit down inside the shrine and meditate there.

The hole was cramped and full of dried sheep poo, but I managed to cram myself in there and then tried to meditate again. At that moment the greeny-blue fly returned and landed on my knee! I was sure it was the same fly I had seen earlier! This time I couldn't ignore him so I tuned in to see what he had to say.

He said he had also been sent by Marielle, the spirit of this place and the spirit of insects. He told me that my task now was to place crystals (quartz points) in springs to cleanse and purify the water and reinvigorate the land. This would prepare the way for 'The coming of the elves'. He also mentioned something about a 'ring of fire' which I did not quite understand.

I was now feeling very uncomfortable and cramped in the hole so I got up and started heading back down into the wooded valley. But I had not gone very far down the hillside before I heard the very faint tinkling sound of running water. I thought I must be imagining it at first but then it grew louder as I found a tiny rivulet flowing through the bracken. “Well where there's water perhaps there's a spring?” I thought, so I followed the tiny rivulet uphill through the bracken until it seemed to emerge from some rocks under a holly bush.

"It couldn't be!" I thought. “I couldn't have found a magical spring so quickly!” But as I pushed back the undergrowth and peered into the shadows, there it was! A perfect little spring flowing out from between two rocks.

The spring was not marked on any maps, I had found it purely through intuition, and now it just so happened that I was carrying some quartz points in my bag! The last time I had found a magic spring I knew I needed a quartz point, though I didn't know why, but at that time I didn't have any, so in the intervening period I had purchased some in case I needed them.

Now that I understood my quest I held the whole batch of crystals in my hand and called upon the power of Merlin to energise them.

The crystals filled with a bright white light which spread to fill my entire body until me and the crystals became one, filled with the same pure energy.

I then placed one of the crystals deep into heart of the spring, at its very source between the rocks, and called upon it to energise the water, then taking out my drinking cup I drank three cupfuls of the clear sparkling water, thereby absorbing its magical energy into my own body.

With my third eye I could see the crystal energising the spring, causing its water to shine with a brilliant white light. This pure white light energy was being carried downstream into the valley, flowing out into the wider world...

Many Roads

March - May

I kept seeing and hearing owls. They were trying to tell me something but I didn't understand and I was not following their guidance.

I sat and meditated by the River Rye in order to try and find out what was going on, and there I was given more guidance about my path and how to release my fears. I was instructed again to place crystals in springs, I was even told which spring I should visit next, but somehow I got side-tracked and did not immediately follow this guidance.

I returned instead to Mulgrave Woods and while visiting the medieval stone castle there I had a flashback from medieval times of peasants and traders passing along the causeway into the castle. As I walked back through the woods I heard a tawny owl hooting, and then I got a text message from a friend. It was an old message I had received before about owls! My phone was playing up and kept sending me this same old message over and over. Strange indeed!

I next visited Thor's Cave in Derbyshire, and then the Neolithic burial chambers of Minninglow where I climbed under an ancient tomb and was visited by a malevolent goblin who seemed to enter my body and drain all my energy, leaving me feeling grey and lifeless. Again I got flashbacks of past lives and then a vision of the dragon from Lake Gormire. "Look at what you have unleashed!" said the goblin. Was he warning me or just trying to scare me? I was feeling slightly lost and afraid. Somehow I just couldn't seem to get back on the right track.

* * *

Next week I visited Glaisdale head, on the North York Moors, a remote moorland valley which has a story about a witch-hare, an old woman who is said to be a witch and can turn into a hare. The hare is shot by a local farmer who chases it to the witches cabin and then finds the old woman inside, wounded!

When I visited the area I could sense the Fae around there but before I left an offering to meet with them I did some dowsing and discovered that they were not friendly. They were dark elves and I was about to make a big mistake by entering their realm! So if I could make a mistake here then where else had I made mistakes? "Look at what you have unleashed!" came into my head again. Now I was really starting to doubt myself!

I continued to explore this remote dale-head, climbing over ancient rockfalls and through twisted forests that clung to the hillside until I came to a glade where a pair of huge gnarly oak trees grew. I left an offering by the oak trees and then decided that this was a good place to tune in and find out more.

I was told again to focus on my mission of placing crystals in springs. I had to put my intention into these crystals so they would cleanse and purify the entire river system. I must also help to connect fairy hills by creating portals between them.

I then left the glade and wandered off into some birches. The birch spirits greeted me and reminded me that if I needed them I need only to call upon them. Then suddenly I spotted an adder!

The snake hissed at me as I approached. Rarely had anyone disturbed him in this remote spot! He puffed his body up and lunged at me when I got too close, so I decided it was best to leave him in peace.

I climbed up through the crags and eventually made it to the edge of the high moor where I found a crow trapped in a cage. He looked terrified but I opened the cage door and stood back while he flapped around and then flew away to freedom, escaping the farmer's revenge. I felt such a sense of joy as I watched him fly away over the dale and I continued to watch as he shrank into a black speck in the distance to begin his new lease of life. They say that crows always remember, so maybe he will remember my act of kindness.

* * *

A few days later I decided to head back up to Scotland so I drove to Traquair and took a walk up onto Minch Moor to visit a fairy spring called the Cheese Well.

I cleared up some mess there and left an offering in a scallop shell. The fairies appreciated this and I could sense them flying all around me. I purified my wand in the spring and was told that my wand had an unwelcome guest. A hobman was hitching a ride in there and should be removed! I then planted my wand in the earth and drew in energy to help heal the fairies, before energising a crystal and placing it in the spring. I waited for the crystal to energise the water before taking a cupful to drink. Strangely the water tasted cheesy!

I then sat down by the well as a fine drizzle started to fall and a beautiful rainbow filled the air, and very soon I fell into a magical trance...

Small elfin spirits appeared with skinny limbs, large heads and pointy hats. The whites of their eyes flashed as they danced around joyfully, energised by the healing I had given them. They took me by the hand and got me to join their dance, and then they started to spin threads around me and wrapped me in a silken cocoon. They rolled me down the hill and took me to see the old owl, the tawny owl. Was he the one who had been trying to contact me all this time?

"You have gone too far down the wrong path," he told me in a wise and refined voice, "You must go back, and find the right path!"

He then grabbed me with his claws and took me high into the air, flying over the countryside!

"Too Woo Too Woo!
You know what to do!
Follow me high over hill and dell.
Too Woo Too Woo!
You know what to do!
Follow this road it will treat you well.

High in the sky,
And deep underground.
Howling wind,
And never a sound!
Down trickling stream,
And deep dark well.
Country lane
And sound of bell."

Speaking in riddles I was getting used to by now, so I didn't try to analyse his words too much, I just accepted the gist of his message. I must find out where I went wrong, and then pick up from there again and find my true path.

The elfin creatures seemed happy now:

"Yippee! Yippee! We've come to take back the world!" they cried.

I felt as if they'd been oppressed for a long time but were finally taking back their freedom.

I opened my eyes from my deep trance and was immediately rewarded with the sight of a bird I'd always wanted to see but had never had the luck to spot before, a beautiful red crossbill! He lingered on the tree opposite for quite some time while I admired him.

As I got up to leave I noticed more 'trash' in the well which I had not noticed before. A small white piece of something. "Odd" I thought, so I picked it up and it was soft and squidgy, like cheese! It made me ponder how this well got its name, The Cheese Well!

I set off back down the hill but before I reached the bottom I remembered I had a little ritual to perform. I went off into the woods and thrust my wand deep into the earth and cast out the unwelcome goblin that I had picked up at Minninglow. He can roam the woods now far from people and hopefully not cause too much trouble!

Later that day I spoke with a psychic called Helen who did some more clearing on me. I did not give her any clues about the kind of things I was into but she had many insights into my past lives, fears and purpose, but most interestingly she told me that I was not originally incarnated as a human but came from another world. Could it be true then, that I came here from the faerie realm?

* * *

My next journey was all the way down to Somerset where I visited Horner Woods near Exmoor. There I encountered a flock of jays which I followed until I lost them deep in the woods where I then heard the bark of a deer. I then continued on and near the head of the dale I found a magical spot where two streams joined.

I knew there was something I had to do there but I couldn't work out what it was, it was something relating to one of the springs. I scouted around and eventually found the problem. A spring had been blocked up and diverted by a local landowner so that it no longer flowed into the valley. Instead there was a stinking stagnant pool full of algae. This was despite it being in a national park and national nature reserve! I took a note of the location and told the environmental protection agency about it later. Walking back through the woods I simply enjoyed the nature and some encounters with wild ponies.

I then returned to my favourite haunt in Somerset, Dundon Beacon with its magical spring and woodland clearing that was like a natural temple. I cleaned up the spring there and spoke with the spirit of the spring.

She told me that by placing quartz crystals in the springs I was amplifying whatever vibration they carried (a bit like homoeopathy!) I must find the springs that were carrying the correct vibration in their waters, and then amplify them.

So I placed a crystal there, in my favourite spring, amplified its energy, and then took a drink of its waters, taking its amplified vibration into my own body!

The next day I went over to Nyland Hill, a perfect conical hill that was once an island, rising from the Somerset levels. I climbed the hill and strolled through the fragrant ramsons (wild garlic) which were in full bloom on this tranquil wooded hilltop.

I could sense elves in the woods there so I sat under an old oak tree and meditated.

The elves appeared and eyed me warily, wondering what I was doing in their woodland. They were lithe and sinewy, with smooth oily skin which was a dark olive green. Their eyes were large, black and slanted. I took out my glowing wand and revealed my true form as Aurvandil, a shining white lord of the Fae! They opened up to me then, and told me that their woodland was now isolated and needed to be connected to other elf woods.

So I called for guidance and was directed to another woodland nearby called Stoke Woods. Once there I found a suitable tree and placed green crystals all around it. I then sat in the tree with my wand and consciously opened a portal between this woodland and Nyland Hill.

As I did so I saw a great arc of white light ascend into the sky and drop back down onto Nyland Hill, like a glowing white rainbow. It felt like the elves could now use this arc of energy as a highway to travel from wood to wood.

As I bent down to pick up my crystals I noticed a small antler poking out of the ramsons. I picked it up and found a complete roe deer skull, perfectly white and picked clean. Another gift from the Fae!

The next day I spoke to Tina and she told me she'd had a vision of me with small antlers on my head, just like on the skull I had found! I was carrying a wooden sceptre in this vision, with a knobbly end. But what did it mean?

* * *

I then headed back home to Yorkshire and finally decided to visit the spring I'd been told about all those weeks ago while sitting by the River Rye!

I travelled to a remote little valley on the North York Moors called Parci Gill. I climbed down into the gill and then followed it upstream where I found a dead rotting sheep lying right in the middle of the flow! It stank to high heaven but I knew I had to remove it as it was polluting all the water, so I grabbed it by the horns and yanked it out, placing it over a tree trunk nearby to dry out.

I then headed further upstream and finally found a little spring bubbling from the ground near a small twisted oak tree.

I tuned in there and received the understanding that I am a changeling! A Fae placed in a human body to carry out a task here on Earth. I am placing crystals in these springs in order to transform the earth into a place more suitable for the fae to inhabit.

So I took another crystal, placed it in this remote spring, and then activated it. As I did so I found myself chanting these lines:

"From the rivulet to the gill
From the gill to the stream
From the stream to the river.
Energising the land.
Purifying it."

Now my path was set for me. Now I was following my guidance again. Now I was back on track at last!

Energising the Sacred Springs of Yorkshire

May - August

Now that I knew what to do my only concern was to find the right springs, but I needn't have worried, because always I am being guided, and the places I am drawn to are usually the places I am meant to be.

My first destination was Rowl Spring on the North York Moors near Levisham. Old and abandoned it lay buried in ramsons and bluebells.

I placed a crystal in the water, blessed it and took a sample of the water in a glass bottle. Suddenly a hoverfly buzzed up to me and sat suspended in the air just in front of me, as it lingered there I tuned in to see if it had a message for me.

I received guidance to visit a chalybeate (iron rich) spring to the north.

After some searching and false leads I eventually found myself hiking along the gully of the Havern Beck towards Newton Dale. Along the way I found a tiny little spring in the wall of the gully. I cleared away the vegetation that hid it and placed a crystal deep in its recesses. I then sipped a cup of the water and a strange otherworldly feeling came over me.

I then continued down the Havern Beck in an otherworldly daze, past a dripping black wall of rock which I named the "Dwarf Door". It felt like an entrance to the Otherworld but my guidance told me not to investigate it further. The whole gully seemed strange and otherworldly somehow, pleasant and natural to look at but somehow sinister. I meditated in a small rock shelter there above a high waterfall but my guides told me to move on.

Eventually I came to the end of the gully and some water meadows. I entered Newton Dale and crossed the tracks of the North York Moors Railway before hiking up a promontory on the other side known as the Needle Eye. A tiny trackway led to Newtondale Spring, a magical hidden place where a constantly flowing stream of water issues forth from the earth over stone steps stained red by the iron-rich water.

I spent a long time tidying up this spring as it had become clogged up with mud, leaves and detritus, my bare feet waded through the thick red sludge as I cleared away a channel for the bright clear water. I waded right up to the source of the spring and placed a crystal deep behind one of the steps before energising it.

I tuned in to get more information and a pattern was now emerging. These springs seemed to have water spirits (nymphs) associated with them, who appreciated their springs being tidied up and looked after. These springs carry a certain energy or vibration which I was amplifying with my crystals. This amplified energy is then carried downstream throughout the entire river system. The energy penetrates the land and affects all those who live there and drink from the water. This new vibration will raise the consciousness of the people, awaken them from their slumber, cause them to question their ways of being and their current beliefs. This is all part of the return of the Fae energy to Earth.

I decided to fill a bottle with this water too. Perhaps it will come in useful sometime? I left an offering of honey there in a scallop shell and gave thanks. By giving this place an air of sacredness my wish was that future visitors would treat this place with the respect and reverence that it deserves and feel its magical energy. It truly was magical there and I wished I could have stayed longer, but dusk was falling and I still had to make it all the way back to my car through the long gully.

* * *

Now I was on a roll, so the next day I headed to Old Wives' Well. It was hidden in the trees near a country lane and not easy to find. I parked in a layby on the remote lane and followed a barely visible track into the trees until I came to a small clearing. Ribbons tied to some of the trees indicated that this place was still revered as a sacred site.

The water in the well was crystal clear but did not seem to be flowing at this time. It did not seem right to energise stagnant water so I took some of the water into a bottle and placed a crystal in the bottle to cleanse it. I then got the message to take the bottle to Brown Howe. I left an offering in a scallop shell that was already provided there and then drove over to Brown Howe which lay in the forest nearby.

Upon arriving I discovered that the howe no longer existed and had been levelled by a local farmer, but I got the farmer to show me the spot nonetheless and took the bottle with me.

There is local folklore associated with Brown Howe which states:

> "To the west of Brown Howe and standing by a boulder there be seen of a summer's eve a maiden there seated a-combing out her jet black tresses so as to hide her bare breast and shoulders, she looking to be much shamed to there do her toilet."

I asked the farmer if he knew of any stories associated with the place but he could only relate that archaeologists had found a jade necklace nearby. I drove away from the farm, parked up nearby and decided to take a shamanic journey to see what I can find out about this place.

I saw myself kneeling down by Old Wives' Well. In my hand was a chalice containing the well water and a crystal. Others were there kneeling around the well with me also holding chalices. Next we were standing around Brown Howe holding our chalices. A great black hole opened up in the ground where the howe used to be. Spirits flew out of the hole and then I dived forward myself into the blackness. I was transported to another world where a beautiful naked woman was lying on a rock. She was combing her long silky black hair and wearing a jade necklace. She removed her necklace and placed it around my neck instead. I saw myself staring into a pool, the jade necklace around my neck was visible in the reflection. Suddenly I recognised where I was, I was by the spring near Obtrush Roque!

It was a convoluted way of getting to the point, but seemingly I should place a crystal there too!

I then met with some of my spirit guides to try to get to know them better, a dirty little 'nut boy', a winged fairy, a lady with a crown of flames and a mermaid. Earth, air, fire and water! I greeted them each in turn, my guides and protectors.

* * *

The next day I went looking for another spring called Old Man's Mouth. I parked in a public car park nearby but somehow managed to miss the spring and ended up climbing through the woods until I found another, less well-known spring which was completely overgrown and clogged up. I spent about an hour digging it out with my bare hands. I discovered old pans and utensils that must have been left there long ago, then some square stone blocks which people likely used to sit on, but eventually I made it down to where the trickle of water actually bubbled from the earth through small pebbles.

I dug out some of the pebbles and placed a crystal deep down in the source of the spring before replacing the pebbles again. I headed back down to the car park, exhausted and then I spotted it! The Old Man's Mouth!

How did I miss it? Closer inspection revealed though that it was not actually a spring, but the outflow of a small rivulet, so there was nothing there for me to energise.

* * *

Following my guidance the next day I headed for the spring near Obtrush Roque that I had seen in my vision. I arrived there in the afternoon but before I could focus on the spring I heard the pathetic bleating of a sheep in the woods nearby. The sheep must have broken out of her field and seemed to be lost, so I opened the gate and chased her into the field. She immediately began munching on the fresh grass, so at least she would not starve!

I did not waste any more time. I lifted a slab to reveal the inflow of the spring and placed a crystal deep inside. I then knelt and stared into the stone basin.

I saw myself as the horned god, with small antlers like the ones I had found in Stoke Wood. I was muscular and strong, with a mossy leotard hanging off one shoulder giving me the appearance of Hercules. I was standing by a giant tree with a tall elf-maiden, her skin was smooth and green like that of a frog. We stepped inside the bark and climbed up high into the branches of the tree and gazed out over a strange and alien land.

I was back in my body again gazing into the pool, but I felt like there was more to discover so I stared some more into the water.

Again I was the horned god, lord of the wildwood. I was standing alone in a clearing in the forest, but slowly animals started to arrive. First a boar, then an owl, then a horse, and then a lone wolf lurking in the shadows. Soon more animals appeared: badgers, deer, foxes, weasels, voles and shrews, all the denizens of the forest. They were soon followed by stranger animals - bears, aurochs and big cats - animals that are now extinct in our land. And finally swarms of insects of every conceivable variety. They gathered in a circle around me. I was the Lord of Animals!

Afterwards I felt strange and spaced out, like I could still feel the horns growing from my skull.

* * *

A few days later I returned to the Lady Keld springs at Cropton, now transformed from winter's chill to the full bloom of spring. But first I explored the area near the old motte where I had previously sensed a Fae energy. Using my dowsing rods to guide me I discovered a hidden glade inside a dense thicket of hawthorn, very close to the motte itself. There was space inside there for a dozen or so people to gather in a circle.

I tuned in and had a vision of travelling faeries gathered there. A large crystal stood in the centre of the clearing and the faeries stood around it, each carrying a crystal-tipped wand which they used to direct energy at the crystal in the centre. I felt myself standing by the crystal, tiny and insignificant, but then I rose up and became Aurvandil, a powerful elf-lord with crystal-tipped wand and blue teardrop necklace. Somehow I was connected to these beings, I was one of them! I then had a vision of a portal elsewhere in the field, a fairy ring, a circular patch of grass that these beings used on occasion to travel between our world and theirs.

I searched the small hidden glade and among the leaves, twigs and rabbit skulls I found an ancient freshwater oyster shell, left here by the Fae long ago. I took it with me, as a momento, unsure as to its purpose.

I continued through the woods and made my way back over the barbed-wire fence that leads to the springs. The waters flowed fast and clear in winter but now in spring the whole gully seemed like one big marsh. I found a very green area of high energy with a little rivulet flowing through it and placed my crystal there.

Immediately the white light started to emanate from the many tiny springs, filling the whole gully with its light. This was different, there were many power centres here, and with one act I seemed to have activated all of them! What a magical experience!

A couple of days later I headed for another spring, this one known as Diana's Well near East Witton. Diana is the Roman goddess of the hunt and has a long association with witches and witchcraft. Now hidden in a private forest the water spewed forth from an ancient carved stone head which was covered with moss. A little well-house and grotto had been built right next to it, and inside the well house at the back I found a stone basin with clear fresh water flowing through it. I placed an energised crystal deep into the inflow and then drank three cups of the water, taking three sips each time; three times three. I sat down by the stone table and immediately an otherworldly feeling came over me. Words came to my lips:

"Spirit of the well
I summon thee forth
You are needed here again
We ask for the spirit of your holy waters"

I then began a long channelling, as if the spirit of the water nymph were speaking through me. It was a long, deep and eloquent speech, but unfortunately I had no way of recording it and could remember afterwards only the main gist of it as follows:

- *You know who you can trust. Trust in yourself most of all.*

- *The world is full of darkness, but while there is light there is hope. Light can spread like wildfire. That is why the darkness is so afraid.*

- *The holy wells are being awakened. People should drink from them and take on the new consciousness they contain.*

- *Dress in white. Gather other lightworkers around you. Promote the holy wells. Cause people to drink their waters. This will bring down a new consciousness to earth, a new light in the darkness, a light that will spread.*

- *You are safe here by Diana's Well and the problems of the outside world will seem far away while you recuperate here.*

I felt like I was my real self in there, a pure shining being with no worries or concerns; calm, relaxed and self-assured. This place was a retreat! A retreat from the greed and destruction that is consuming our world.

But I was not done yet! I visited a couple more springs that day before making my way to a place called the Fairy Well near Harmby.

The Fairy Well is a natural spring that sits on the slope of a grassy field where locals often walk their dogs, and it is overlooked by magical hawthorn trees, fairy thorns.

When I arrived there the hawthorn trees were in full bloom, covered in enchanting white flowers that signal the arrival of summer in the old Celtic calendar. I rooted through the boulders at the base of one the hawthorn trees until I found the source of the spring and then placed my crystal deep inside. I felt that this place had lost some of its ancient magic and needed revitalising. In my mind's eye I saw mysterious lights twinkling in the mist around these trees at dusk, and I invited the fairies back in there and wished for magical happenings that would spark the interest of the locals again and reawaken the mystical properties of this place.

* * *

A couple of days later I travelled with my friend Liz to find more springs. As on previous days I found a couple of springs that turned out to be unsuitable for energising, but eventually we made our way to the village of Hackness and crossed a field full of bullocks to find St. Hilda's Spring, hidden inside the edge of the forest.

We came to a large pool that looked clear and unpolluted, though rather clogged with fallen branches.

A concrete sump had been built in the centre of the pool, out of which flowed a descent volume of water which roared as it emerged from the far side of the pathway. Well if water is leaving the pool then it must be entering somewhere! I could see water trickling into the pond on the far side, so there was nothing for it but to wade in and take a closer look! In the far left corner I found the main inflow. The moss around the spring had turned to stone, so clearly this water had petrifying properties.

I placed my crystal, energised the water, and then drank it directly from its source, three cups of three sips. I was then told that I should return here at a later date.

That evening I felt completely drained and exhausted. A feeling I had felt many times after energising these sacred springs. Was this work draining my energy? Or was it just the icy cold chill of the water?

* * *

Nevertheless a few days later I was heading for another spring! This time it was Waterhouse Well at Rosedale Abbey. This well, which was once used by the monks of the abbey, was now located in a caravan park, but still sat in its old purpose-built well house.

I cleared out some rubbish and detritus that had collected in there and then sat down by the clear, fresh spring inside.

I placed a crystal deep inside the spring and then tuned in to the energies there. But this time I got a surprise!

I felt a small imp shoot out of the well and enter my body! I shuddered and opened my eyes. I had made a mistake this time! I had gotten lazy and didn't check first to see if this was one of the springs I should be energising. I tried to move the imp on, but he was stuck there inside me. Still, I had probably done a good thing by removing the imp from the well, but I did not feel that this was the task I was here to perform.

I took back my crystal as it felt like it was not meant to be there, and then set off to explore the rest of Rosedale. I drove right up to the end of the dale and then took an ancient trackway back down the far side of the valley through many lush green fields and old gateways.

I finally arrived at the quaint little village of Thorgill on the far side of the valley, bright with spring flowers and lush gardens. I followed a little beck upstream through the gill (a gill is an indentation in the hillside created by a small stream), high up onto the moors, until I reached its source above at Thorgill Head. After much searching I found the place where the water emerged directly from the earth, gushing forth in a steady stream. Relieved I placed my crystal there and energised it, and then watched as the energy flowed down from the high moor, through the gill and into the populated valley below.

Loch Maree: The Queen of Fairies Island

23rd August

In the remote North West corner of Scotland there is a large loch, which nowadays goes by the name of Loch Maree. It is said that on that loch there is an island, and within that island there is another small hidden loch, and on that loch there is yet another island. An island within an island within an island! A legendary place where on certain nights of the year the queen of the fairies is said to hold court.

After some research I discovered that the island containing the small loch is called Eilean Subhain and it is the largest island on Loch Maree. But even more intriguing to me was a nearby island called Isle Maree. The island contained an ancient burial ground which dated back to the time of the druids, and it also held a wishing tree, a druid circle and a holy well. It was also known for its bull sacrifices which continued until the 17th century. So off I headed Northwards across the border to this remote part of Scotland to investigate!

I arrived to find that the hotel on the edge of the loch was closed. I met there with the manager who told me he'd had to close for the whole year due to numerous burst pipes and water damage caused by last year's severe winter. It seemed like an ill fated place, a string of bad fortune had seen a previous manager commit suicide (he was later buried on Isle Maree). Despite all this, the current manager still seemed like a jolly chap and offered to take me over to the islands in his boat.

We set off across the lake and passed Eilean Subhain on our left, barren looking and dotted with pines, and then Isle Maree slowly came into view ahead, a lush oasis of thick oaks said to have been planted there by the druids. The island is unique, the Scots pines that cover all the other islands are absent here, replaced by oak and holly and other hardwoods.

He dropped me at the shingle beach on this small island and then he headed back to shore, leaving me alone and stranded in the middle of this great loch.

The island was no more than a hundred metres across and seemed to be composed entirely of small rounded stones. Man made perhaps? Or the remains of a glacial moraine? Several theories have been put forward but none have satisfactorily explained this strange little island.

I headed off on a small track that led up from the beach and soon came to the remains of the famous money tree, studded with old coins left there by countless pilgrims from times gone by, including Queen Victoria herself!

Near the money tree was said to lie a holy well, once famous for its lunacy cure. The unfortunate patient had to be carried around the island three times in a boat, each time being dunked in the sea, before heading to the well to drink its curing waters and spending the night on the island. But unfortunately the well has long ago been filled in and there is now no trace left of it at all.

Higher up on the island, to my left, I could make out some gravestones and so went over to investigate and soon came to a low stone wall which formed a complete a circle, about twenty metres in diameter. This was the famous 'druid' circle which had lain here since ancient times and was likely constructed by the Picts for ritual purposes.

I walked around the edge of the circle, not wanting to enter yet. Isle Maree had seemed like a magical place when viewed from the outside, but now that I was in the heart of the island it seemed rather forbidding. I avoided entering the circle at first, but after wandering around the rest of the island I eventually decided to make my way in.

I soon came upon two graves said to have belonged to earlier Viking settlers. They were simple slabs of stone set into the ground and carved with ancient Celtic crosses in a crude style. The legend concerning their death is a tragic one. The first grave belongs to Olaf, who killed himself when he thought that his truelove had died. The second grave belongs to her, she killed herself when she realised her terrible folly, pretending to be dead to test her hero's love.

I thought that I had come to this island to find the holy well, but being able to find absolutely no trace of it left me wondering why I came here. I suddenly felt compelled to lie down on top of Olaf's grave slab and meditate there.

I felt Olaf's spirit enter me. Was he looking for his lost love? No, he seemed to be more concerned about a pot of gold he had buried and not been able to retrieve before he died! Well so much for legends...

Even in the spirit world this island seemed grey and forbidding, a place of sacrifice. I felt my spirit rise up into the sky, ascending higher and higher. I looked down upon the loch and saw Isle Maree, a grey and ghostly speck with its stone circle in the centre looking like an ancient sun-wheel (a cross within a circle). I then looked across and saw the larger island of Eilean Subhain, also looking ghostly in the twilight, but within it I could see a small glowing island of glittering golden light! Yes, that's where I had to go, that's what had drawn me here! I had become too distracted by the myths and legends of Isle Maree!

Suddenly I felt a piercing stab! I was back in my body lying on the grave slab and saw a bull-headed man standing over me thrusting a spear into my belly!

I quickly cast the vision away and belatedly placed some protections around myself. I then rose from the slab a bit shocked and shaken.

Is this why this island was famous for its bull sacrifices? Were they sacrificing to this spirit? I later discovered that highlanders were known for wearing bull skins over their heads when performing rituals, had I perhaps met the spirit of one of these ancient shamans who still protected the island?

I took a final wander around the shores of the island while I waited for the boatman to return, gazing across at the remote hillsides on the Northern shore of Loch Maree that were covered in ancient scots-pines.

When the boatman arrived he showed me something that I had missed. The remains of a stone-lined channel ran north-south, right across the centre of the druid circle, and over it lay a stone slab where it was said that the bull sacrifices had taken place.

If there was another channel running east-west then the circle would indeed form the sunwheel that I had seen in my vision!

The boatman then ferried me over to Eilean Subhain and dropped me off in a sheltered bay on the Northern shore of the island, my plan being to trek across the island, investigate the loch, and then meet the boatman later in the evening on the southern shore of the island. I heard the boatman's engine chug away into the distance and was then left in perfect silent isolation on this rugged island.

The ground was rough and boggy as I made my way south across the island to the place where I believed that the small inner loch might lay.

After a while I ascended a rise in the land and suddenly there it was, a lake where no lake ought to be! This was not part of Loch Maree, but a hidden nameless loch secreted away on this small island.

But before I could stop to admire the view I noticed movement in the water. It was an otter... and he had just caught a fish!

He carried the fish onto a tiny island within the loch and disappeared into the heather, but I could hear him crunching away on his fish, crunch, crunch, crunch! I crept up as close as I could to the island, and instinct led to me to a spot where I crouched down waiting for him to emerge. He did not disappoint me...

He had no idea that I was sitting just a few feet away from him! I could have watched his antics all day, but I had come here for another reason... As I got up the otter swam away to the other side of the lake, hunting for more fish. The island where the otter had eaten his fish looked like a likely place, but the boatman had specifically told me that the fairy queen's island could be waded to, and the water between me and this small island was too deep. But there was another island I could see near the opposite shore of the lake, so off I plodded through the rough heather, hoping to make it around to the far side.

The heather and grasses seemed to be full of a multitude of insects, especially brightly coloured dragonflies and damselflies that were so placid I could actually walk right up to them and stroke their wings!

After trekking over the rough ground I finally made it to a stand of tall pines that I had seen from the opposite shore, and then the final stretch over some very boggy terrain that threatened to suck my boots off! Then I made it to the small channel that separated the tiny island from the shore where I stood.

It was time to take off my boots and start wading! So eventually, without too much difficulty, I made it across onto the rough heather that covered this tiny knoll. So was this it? Was this the fairy queen's island?

I climbed to the highest point of the small island and stood where I imagined the faerie queen's throne ought to be.

I instantly felt the flutter of huge dragonfly wings beside me. It was the Faerie Queen! She stood there with flowing golden hair and flowing orange dress as if being swept by an invisible wind. She summoned forth a swarm of insects from the wilderness all around! Glittering dragonflies, butterflies, bees and beetles of all shapes, sizes and colours. All the wild nature from the land around seemed to be drawn to her. The insects and other flying creatures coalesced around her and formed into a giant whirling vortex. They then suddenly spread out all over the land, carrying with them a magical energy.

As I watched the vision these words came forth unbidden from my lips:

"You will sit on your throne again
Your magic throne
Lady of the beasts
Lady of the wild
Come take back your throne
The animals await
They're at your command
They're here to do your bidding
Lady of nature
The animals are at your command
Queen of nature
Retake your throne my lady
My lady of nature
The animals approach
The animals are coming here
Great stirrings in the Earth

A time of change and reckoning
Swarms and swarms swarming
Carried on a whirlwind
A portal opens from above
A gate to the Otherworld
They're coming through
They've been waiting for this day
The Shining Ones return to Earth!"

I watched as a golden portal opened in the sky above me, and golden winged beings stepped down a glittering staircase onto the surface of the lake. They formed a glowing row of bright, celestial, winged beings spread out in a line right across the lake, their huge wings spread, almost touching tip to tip, as they gazed skywards...

What could this mean? Who were these 'shining ones'? I opened my eyes and was once more alone and back in the wild nature of Scotland. In a daze I climbed down and waded back from the little island. I put on my boots and continued across the main island, heading further south.

I walked through some odd, almost prehistoric looking terrain of shaped and eroded rocks until I came to a second lake, which if anything looked even more magical than the first!

I had some time alone there before the boatman arrived, so I lay on a spit of grass surrounded by water and tried to meditate again, but instead I pondered what had drawn me here to this remote island. Was I calling in the Goddess and activating the nature spirits, preparing them for a time soon to come when they could repopulate the land once more? And who were these shining ones? They seemed like they came from another planet or another dimension!

* * *

When I got back to civilisation I went online and did some research into 'the shining ones' to try to find out who they could be, but there seemed to be no simple answers. I read about the sons of Horus, Hindu devas, Roman and Celtic sun gods, and about the elves of Norse mythology, but nothing sounded very satisfactory, so I dug around a while more and finally came up with an article that seemed to resonate more deeply, it described the "Mighty Shining Ones" as the Elohim, the "ancient teachers of mankind."

Iona, St Columba and the Well of Age

28th August

I was drawn to the sacred island of Iona in Scotland for several reasons, for its holy wells and fairy sites, and for its associations with mysticism and prophetic visions. Iona had been a holy island since ancient times, even before the Celtic saint Columba travelled there from Ireland and set up one of Britain's earliest Christian missions, way back in the 6th century.

I started by climbing Dun I, Iona's highest hill, to look for the fabled Well of Age, also known as the Well of Healing or the Fountain of Youth. It is said that if you splash the water on your face at sunset it will "roll back the years", but it is also known as a vision site by mystics. St. Bridget (who is the Christian version of the Celtic goddess Bride) is said to have climbed Dun I, and after rescuing a lamb from a falcon at the Well of Age she drank the water and had a vision. She stepped through a magical gateway created by two rowan trees and was transported back to the birth of Jesus by two angels to act as midwife!

The climb to the top was easy enough, but at first I could not find the pool, only a small puddle under a rock. So I got my dowsing rods out to find out if I was in the right place, and after asking a few questions I turned around and there it was! A large pool perched upon the edge of a cliff.

The wind was blowing up there making quite a din, but as I climbed down to the edge of the pool all was calm and quiet. I sat by the pool in that sheltered spot and splashed the water onto my eyes, then sat down and meditated as the cold water slowly evaporated from my face.

I could sense small playful elfin creatures dancing and playing around the pool and then a portal opened at the back of the pool with stairs going down under the rock. I walked down and soon found myself in a beautiful passageway, with an ivory, arched colonnade to my left through which I could see the most breathtaking trees covered all over in bright pink blossoms. I knew that I was back in Elfland. Walking with me on my right was an elven lady wearing a long white dress with long flowing golden hair.

"It is always spring in Elfland", she said, "If you wish it to be!"

I knew that I was being tempted to stay, and the place was so beautiful and calming that the temptation was great indeed, but I also knew that I had a job to do on Earth, and no matter how difficult my life on Earth might become, I had to complete whatever I had come here for before I could return to the Otherworld.

Without a word, but with a knowing look of calm serenity she led me further down the stairs to a high colonnaded courtyard containing the most majestic and awe-inspiring tree I had ever seen. Its perfectly formed branches shone golden, holding aloft a perfect crown of leaves which gave off a golden light. Amongst them were nestled a sparkling array of lights like glowing gems of all shapes and colours that twinkled in the twilight.

"This is the tree of knowledge", she said, "but it is sick. You must heal our tree."

I knew that she meant there was something I must do on Earth in order to help heal the tree, but what that was I could not comprehend.

As the vision faded I heard a voice say: "Come back at midnight and drink the water".

Afterwards everything felt otherworldly, like I was seeing our world superimposed upon a world that lies hidden beneath, a world somehow more real and vibrant than our own world.

I descended Dun I, down the far side that led towards the centre of the island. My next destination was the Hermit's Cell, a place of "spiritual wish-fulfilment and mystical experiences" where Robert Ogilvie-Crombie had met with the god Pan, and many other people have had visions and unusual experiences.

After struggling across the rough and trackless terrain for about an hour I finally spotted some low stone walls by a large rocky outcrop, and from the descriptions I had read I knew that I had found the right place.

I climbed to the top of the rocky outcrop to survey area from above. To my right was a square enclosure incorporating huge boulders that looked like they could have been ancient monoliths from prehistoric times.

To my left I could clearly make out the small stone circular enclosure of the Hermit's cell, also known as "Tigh nan Cuildich" The House of the Culdees, looking like a strange stone ulcer on the surface of the land.

I climbed down from my hilltop eminence, circled slowly around the cell, and then stood by the entrance and closed my eyes.

I could feel the energy emanating from the cell. Within it a column of yellow light reached up to the sky and was filled with flickering golden tendrils that extended to the heavens. I stepped inside and basked for a while in the incredible energy. It soon made me feel very spaced out! The energy seemed to be beaming down from an extra-terrestrial source as if it came from a flying saucer suspended in the sky. I felt myself being lifted up in the energy, growing taller and taller, until I was a huge being, like an ancient god, the Lord of All Wild Things. I looked down upon Iona from above and could see the Hermit's Cell at the centre, the omphalos of the island, it's centre of power.

I returned to my body and lay down in the cell, the energy then formed a dome over me and I lay there feeling very otherworldly, in a deeply meditative state, until I was no longer aware of my own body. I felt like I was floating in a dream.

Eventually I arose and walked back to the large square enclosure by the cliff. I found a deep crevice in the rock face and squeezed in there with my back to the rock, facing the landscape of Iona. There I meditated even deeper and released some of my deep-seated needs which I realised were focused too much on this material world. I had no need to prove myself or justify myself, for a while at least I could just be.

I walked back to the village by a long and boggy route, slightly lost my way, and then was attacked by an angry dog in a farmyard! Luckily he was on a long lead so I managed to jump out of his reach, just in time!

Back at my B&B I looked up the "Tree of Knowledge" on the internet and found out that it was the tree from the Hebrew bible from which Adam and Eve took the forbidden fruit. But the real meaning of this allegorical tale seems to be that the tree represents the knowledge that first separated mankind from the animals. We chose to become different from the other creatures in this world by eating of this 'forbidden' knowledge. It also seems to be linked to the advent of farming somehow, as Adam and Eve's descendants were farmers, no longer in complete harmony with nature but struggling against it. Another reference to the "ancient teachers of mankind" maybe?

* * *

I returned to Dun I later that evening in total darkness. There was no moon or stars, and the wind was whipping in from the sea, rattling wires and fences. Everything looked dark and spooky, some scarecrows by a vegetable patch had a demonic appearance and even a collection of garden gnomes clustered around someone's doorstep had a sinister aspect. After passing through the village I set off up the trackless hillside in complete darkness, with only the light of my weak head-torch to guide my way through the surrounding blackness. I could just make out the grey outline of Dun I in the darkness and so I headed in that direction, trying to avoid slipping into a bog or some treacherous hole in the ground. As my route started to get steeper and steeper I thought I must be crazy to be doing this! I persevered nonetheless, but did not like it one bit!

Eventually I reached the summit with its cairn of stones, and was immediately blasted by a howling gale blowing in from the far side of the hill! The roar of the wind, the darkness and my small cone of light was all that I was aware of. I struggled over the top of the hill and made my way down to the Well of Age, which was taking the full blast from the onshore wind. Climbing down into rocks by the pool did not offer much protection, and the black surface of the well was being pummelled by the air as it crashed into the rock face, creating a constant rippling effect on the surface of the pond like it was being blasted by a giant hair-dryer.

I sat there and tried to relax. Turning off my torch I could see lights twinkling on the rock face and saw blurry patches of otherworldly shadow passing over it that never quite coalesced into recognisable forms, but I could sense the presence of spirits there nonetheless. I closed my eyes and tried to relax in the howling darkness, but it was no use. As I opened my eyes I noticed that it had got even darker. It started to rain. Clearly this was not the place to be right now!

I decided to make my way back down the hill, stumbling in the darkness. I imagined what it must have been like living there long ago, in the darkness, when the land was populated by malevolent spirits intent upon trickery and luring people to their deaths; urisks, mermaids, selkies, the sidhe and the walking dead. How superstitious and terrified people must have been on nights like this! What a comfort it must have been when the Christian missionaries arrived offering people the protection of God and the saints, and the sanctuary of the church. Is it any wonder that people decided to convert to Christianity?

I was glad to make it back to the relative safety of the village. As I wandered past the ancient abbey I noticed a flickering red light coming from a tiny window in the door of St. Oran's chapel. It looked warm and comforting so I decided to investigate. I pushed the door and it was open, so I stepped inside. The chapel was lit by the warm glow of a single red candle sat on the altar, its light reflected by a polished steel Celtic cross set above it, which illuminated the tombstones of old Highland chieftains that were set into the walls.

It seemed like a place of peace, contentment and spirituality, carrying none of the heavy energy I usually associated with churches. I sat on one of the benches and soaked up the air of calm serenity as I watched the flickering glow of the candle dancing over the walls.

I closed my eyes and sensed a cowled figure step out from the corner of the room, his hand held up in a blessing. Was this St. Columba? He told me that I had come to Iona seeking spirituality, like so many others before me. He said that I should stop chasing spirits (fairies) and serving them, and that what I really sought was my own spirituality. "Spirituality not wizardry" was his message to me. He then anointed my forehead with oil.

Feeling calmed by the experience I left the chapel and headed back to my lodgings.

* * *

The next day as I sat eating breakfast I could see dolphins swimming in the strait of water that separated Iona from the mainland. They were leaping out of the water and playing as a yacht sailed by them. What a great way to start the day!

After my experience of the night before I decided to visit the abbey. There was something about the Celtic church which interested me, it was not like the stuffy old churches I had been brought up with in England but seemed to be more closely linked to our spiritual and pagan past somehow.

I sat in St. Columba's tiny shrine and started to meditate there when the caretaker suddenly stepped inside the door. He had come to clean the bird droppings off the walls which were deposited there by the nesting swallows. The very moment he told me this a swallow flew in, fluttered past our heads, and dropped into its nest above us! The swallows, already late for their southerly migration, only added to the magic of the place.

I wandered around the rest of the abbey and took note of all the ancient grave slabs of Scottish chieftains which had been moved in here from the graveyard to preserve them.

A Sunday service was going on in the main hall, and the ethereal singing would have created a perfect enchantment were it not for all the gaudily dressed, camera-touting tourists wandering around.

I decided I'd had enough of this tourist circuit for now and so I headed out to the next place on the island I wished to visit; Sithean Mor, 'The Large Fairy Mound'. This was the location where legend records that St. Columba had been seen communing with a host of glowing angels. I was intrigued by this story and wondered what St. Columba had been up to on this mound.

The wind was howling again as I made my way across country down a little lane. I found the fairy mound in a field by the lane, it was part of a farm called Sithean, which is Scots-Gaelic for 'Fairy Mound'!

I had intended to sit on top of the mound and see what I could tune into there, but I was being buffeted so badly by the wind that I decided to sit facing the mound in the shelter of a nearby mound known as Sithean Beg 'The Little Fairy Mound.'

I took myself back in time and saw St. Columba wandering over to the mound, his hand clasping a knobbly staff. He looked more like a druid than a priest, and it occurred to me that perhaps that was, in a way, what he was. A druid who also followed Christ. As he reached the top of the mound, a host of shining white beings descended from 'heaven' and then consorted with the saint.

Were these the Shining Ones again? The secret teachers of mankind who reveal themselves only to a select few? The record states that St. Columba was annoyed about being spied upon when he communed with these beings, and punished the priest who did so. So who are these Shining Ones? Are they angels, fairies, or extra-terrestrials? Perhaps these beings, wherever they came from, are the basis for all of these strange beliefs and legends? And what of the druids? Did they really die out, or did they become the priests of the Celtic church preserving ancient knowledge?

These were questions I would not find the answers to today. It was time for me to leave the sacred island, knowing that the answers to these riddles must lie elsewhere.

St Blane's Church and The Fairy Well

29th August

The ruins of St. Blane's Church lie on the site of an ancient monastery, one of the first of its kind in the British Isles. The walls of the monastery and the foundations of some of the ancient monks' cells still exist in this secluded woodland location near the southern tip of the Isle of Bute in Scotland.

I was drawn to this place because of its healing fairy well and a strange circular enclosure called the Devil's Cauldron which archaeologists could find no real explanation for. Folklore tells that within the Devil's Cauldron once grew a pine tree that had the magical power to give visions if a sprig of its leaves were left under one's pillow overnight.

I drove down from Iona and arrived at St. Blane's Church in the light of early evening, the air felt clear and the sky was bright and breezy. Luckily the place was deserted so I had it all to myself! The layout of the site was impressive, with the vallum (wall) that enclosed the original sixth century monastery site still clearly visible and marking the boundary of this ancient and sacred place.

I could also see the ruins of the twelfth century church ahead, but I ignored the ruined church for now and headed straight for the fairy well, but when I got there I was disappointed to discover that a very heavy iron grille had been placed over it, set permanently into concrete.

To me this was a desecration, it violated the spirit of the place. But at least the well was still there, even if it did now have to be viewed through iron bars, and it still gave off a certain sparkly energy.

I next went over to the Devil's Cauldron. It no longer had a pine tree growing in it, or any trees growing nearby. Perhaps those eager for visions had destroyed the pine tree long ago by taking too many sprigs? Now it was just filled with cropped grass and a few rocks, but it had a certain energy that made me wary about entering, it felt somehow powerful, glowing and golden. I did some protections and then stepped through the entrance.

Inside it was filled with golden light, and I could see an even brighter light coming from a large being that stood inside there. It was a strange 'alien' creature, with a long head and long arms, and it stood stooping over me. I reached out to touch its long fingers, but it was like trying to touch a mirage, I was not able to communicate with it at all.

I stepped back outside the Cauldron and noticed many primrose leaves growing nearby. I picked thirteen of them and rubbed them into my wand so that the juice stained the runes on there. Primroses are known from folklore to be a way to open doors to the otherworld, so my intent was to infuse my wand with this ability.

I next decided to get out my dowsing rods and I dowsed an energy line going into and out of the Cauldron, but when I stepped inside the Cauldron to follow the line it formed a spiral going in to the centre. This was definitely some kind of power node, a place of power and a place of visions. So I decided to lay down inside the cauldron and see where it would take me.

I was accompanied by a power animal that had been lurking around in the background for a while now, but who I'd never quite got acquainted with. It was a blue-eyed silver wolf. He took me to a crystal cave where a wise old bearded man awaited, some kind of god-like spirit guide. He showed me that the cauldron was a place of power, glowing with yellow energy, and he showed me the sparkly white energy coming from the well.

This is the reason why the monks chose this place and built a wall around it all. They wanted to harness the energy of this place and use it for their own ends, to employ its power and to have spiritual experiences and visions. These monks were more like druids than churchmen! But over the generations these powers were forgotten as the monks became more orthodox.

I was told that I should venerate the well, and focus my intention there to make it become a sacred and magical place once more.

I got up from the cauldron, feeling rather spaced out, and headed back over to the well.

I took a quartz crystal out of my bag and held it in my hand.

"With this crystal I hereby place my intention
That this place shall once again be venerated.
It shall become a holy place,
A magic place,
That folk will flock to
To worship
And receive healing, joy and happiness."

I placed the crystal into the well and then took out a corn dolly which I had bought in Glastonbury. I attached it to the metal grill so that people would know this was a special place.

"Let the magic flow forth
Flow forth from this holy well
Let it light up the sky
Let it draw folk here from far and wide
Its magic shall flow out
Flow out over the land
Cascading
Drawing people here
Bringing the joy of nature
And Mother Earth to all
They will dance and sing and tie ribbons
Soon they will come
They will feel the magic
It will enter them
A place of ceremony and celebration
A new paganism
A new spirituality
Filled with joy and love
I will make this happen!
Old institutions will crumble

All shall be enlightened, renewed and refreshed
So mote it be!"

I felt like my work was done here at last, so I wandered around this peaceful and enchanted spot in the late evening light enjoying the nature and the atmosphere of the place.

St Anne's Well, Trellech, Fairy Frogs

31st October

It felt like my task in Scotland was completed, so now the time had come for me to enter another Celtic land, the land of Merlin Emrys, Wales!

I began my investigation of the faery lore of Wales, by heading to St. Anne's Well, Trellech, in the south-east corner of Wales near Monmouth.

St Anne's Well is a healing well, which is also known as the Virtuous Well. Its name has been Christianised so originally it was associated with the Celtic deity Annis, goddess of waters, wells and wisdom. St. Anne's well is also said to be the haunt of fairies, who come here each midsummer's eve to dance around the well and drink from harebell cups.

I arrived there on a dull, wet, Samhain-eve (31st October), cursing the foul weather. Having just come back from the hot deserts of Arizona (see appendix) I gave thanks for the rain anyway, remembering the life and vitality it brings to our land, but wondering if we really need so much of it!

The well lay in a field just by the road and is easily accessed. I could see the clootie rags tied to the trees nearby and could just make out the stone outline of the well. I stepped inside the stone enclosure and saw many more offerings lying in alcoves and around the well. I approached the central alcove which contained the well and peered down into the murky water. It looked stagnant and not a trickle could be heard.

I left an offering in a scallop shell and tied a silk clootie rag to the tree. It was not an inspiring day, but the drizzle was easing off so I got my dowsing rods out to try to get some information.

The message I got was that this water carried a vibration I needed and I should drink it!

Putting off the idea of dipping my cup into the murky water I sat down under the trees to meditate instead, but as I did so I noticed a small frog in the grass.

"I bet you like the rain!" I said.

It made me realise that while I was cursing the rain, others were thriving in it and needed it for their very survival. That made me feel a bit more humble.

"Are you the guardian of this place?" I asked.

I picked up Mr. Frog and held him in my hands, but he didn't like it and immediately leaped off.

As he did so I got the feeling like he was leaping down my throat! I could then hear my voice speaking with the voice of the frog, I literally had a frog in my throat!

"Drink the water!" said his froggy voice.

"Oh no! Not that again," I thought.

As the frog sat there in front of me I closed my eyes and meditated.

I followed the frog into the otherworld and he showed me a vision of the fairies dancing in a circle around the well. They looked like children wearing white shifts with flowers in their hair. I wanted to see more, I wanted to know why I was here, but he had nothing more to show me.

I bade him farewell and returned to the well, drinking cup in hand. I peered down into the water. It was dark, deep and still, but I could just make out the bottom, which meant that the water couldn't be that murky, could it?

"Oh well, here goes!" I thought.

I scooped up some water and pondweed. It looked surprisingly clear, so I took a sip, and then another and another. It went down nicely, as did the small pieces of pondweed! After the third sip I opened my eyes and was astonished by what I saw! A big frog looking back up at me from the depths of the pool! There was no doubt about it, this was real magic!

“He must be the guardian of the pool, like the salmon that guards magic pools in Irish legends”, I thought.

He was swimming around helplessly against the side of the well, but how did he get in, and how could he possibly get out? The well was over a foot deep from the rim to the waterline and there was absolutely no way to jump out! A magic frog indeed if he can simply materialise in this well!

I thought I would help him so I placed my hand under him, fully expecting him to struggle and squirm, but he just lay there contentedly as I picked him up and placed him gently in front of the well opening.

I sat and looked at him, and he sat and looked back at me.

"Do you mind if I take your photo?" I said. I didn't hear him object, so I went to fetch my camera and took a photo of him.

So what was I to do now? Was he a messenger from the fairies? Did he have a task for me? Did he want me to follow him?

I took some crystals and other items from my bag to try to get a clue, but he showed his disapproval by crawling back inside the well-house and sitting in a crevice in there.

"You take a lot of photos," he said.

"I like to show people what I've been doing," I replied.

"Release that need," he said.

He was right, I was worrying too much about keeping records and informing people, and I was getting distracted by this. I had been away from my homeland too long and had been focusing on the wrong things.

"Switch off your mind," he said.

I knelt down in front of the well and meditated deeply. I pushed my head in through the small entrance and seemed to pass through a veil into another world.

Soon I was in a world of huge gnarled old oaks, black and damp from the rain. The frog was ahead of me leaping through the wet twisted roots and so I jumped onto his back. We were in the underworld, the old world of nature and spirits where we came from before we entered this modern world.

"Use your intuition," he said.

I opened my eyes and then noticed a half-burned joss stick (incense stick) poking from the earth right in front of him.

"Light it!"

I got my lighter out and lit it, fully expecting him to reel from the flames, but he just sat there impassively, staring.

First I placed the joss stick outside the well, but then amazingly another tiny frog appeared as if from nowhere, jumping out of the well and past the joss stick! Now I had seen three sizes of frogs; medium frog, big frog and now tiny frog! I placed the burning joss stick back in the well and knelt down to meditate some more. What was going on I wondered?

I was immediately carried away on the heady scent of the incense stick, to the spicy land of India. I had visions of deserts, towering dunes, mystical cities, intricately carved temples and exotic robes. I could feel myself back there in India and I was loving it! Did I have to return there someday? The idea had been in the back of my mind for some time now.

I opened my eyes again. Big frog was still sitting there impassively in his crevice, throat oscillating with a regular rhythm.

"Thanks Mr. Frog," I said.

I sat down on the stone bench beside the well and took out a glittering purple stone which I use for releasing negative energies and emotions.

I called upon archangel Zadkiel and felt the whole chamber fill with a violet flame from the heavens. I released the need to record my discoveries, my need to share my findings with others, the need to convince others, and anything else that was holding me back from getting into the flow of my own true path, all the fears and pressures of this physical world.

I could see my path unfolding before me and the freedom was exhilarating! The freedom to pursue my own destiny! 'The Virtuous Well' was showing me the virtuous path!

And now that I had released the *need* to record all this information I could actually enjoy doing it again!

As dusk fell I went to visit the nearby trio of standing stones that gave the village of Trellech its name. The waters of the spring are said to run under the standing stones which themselves are linked with ancient druidic rites. I could just make out the huge standing stones across the field in the dwindling twilight and then I heard the loud screeching and hooting of a pair of owls nearby.

I saw a fluttering near the top of the right hand stone. One of the owls perhaps? I walked around the stones in darkness and placed my hands on the central one. It seemed to be pointing up towards the stars. Were they ancient reminders of a long lost technology and civilization, or just a monument to the vanity of mankind? Maybe this was why I was not overly drawn to standing stones, perhaps they were symbols of mankind's earlier attempts to manipulate the forces of nature? Springs were entirely natural, the creation of the goddess, standing stones were not, they were planted there by mankind, linking earth and sky, the above with the below.

Samhain-eve is the magical night when the veil between the worlds is thinnest, but now it was cold, dark and wet. The frogs had nothing more to show me this evening, it was time to seek shelter and warmth.

Craig y Ddinas Fairy Fort

2nd November

The Vale of Neath in South Wales has long been held to be a place of enchantment and has produced many tales regarding the fairy folk. The central place of enchantment in the whole valley is the fairy fort of Craig y Ddinas, said to have been the last stronghold of the fairies in Wales.

I arrived there on an early November afternoon under an overcast sky. The minor road through the village of Pontneddfechan led over a bridge to a small car park right at the base of the craggy hill. A couple of climbers wearing hard hats were scaling one of the rock faces, while another rock face had been completely covered over in a wire mesh, presumably to avert rockfalls. This was disappointing, I was hoping to have the place to myself, and I was sure that the fairies did not appreciate the metal covering that had been attached to their hill!

I avoided the climbers and managed to find a small trail to the right that seemed to lead right up the side of the hill. As I crept up, the path got steeper and the rocks became more slippy, until eventually I was climbing on all fours, hauling myself up the side of the crag through narrow gaps in the rocks or around precipitous ledges.

With relief I made it to the top and admired the spectacular view. It was then that I noticed that this rocky promontory sat in a fork between two rivers that joined together just beyond the car park. These liminal places in the fork between two rivers are especially magical, and this was the most magical of such places I had ever been to! I could clearly hear the roaring of the rivers deep below in the wooded gorges on either side of me.

Closing my eyes I stood there on the summit of this high windy place and tuned in to the energies.

I was immediately transported to the face of the cliff, just in front of where I was standing. Floating there in mid-air I saw a fairy door open in the cliff face before me, so after a slight hesitation I stepped inside.

The interior of the hill contained a rabbit-warren of dark corridors populated by elves in dark shiny armour, who all seemed to be preoccupied, either going about their business or just standing there as if on guard. I didn't find anyone to talk to and soon found myself transported back outside to the summit where my physical body was still standing.

My guide Atheron was there, he too was one of the 'dark elves'. He told me to link this fort to the others, as I had done oftentimes before.

"The dark elves are hidden here, not departed," he told me. "Connect them to the web!"

I raised my wand over my head and did as I was instructed, bringing down the pure white energy from the sky, conducting it through my own body, and down into the ground through my feet where it entered the chambers below me. The energy then spread out in many directions on beams of white light, connecting this fort with all the other high places I had visited, both in this land and in others, linking it in to the web of light which now seemed to cover the entire earth.

Then I remembered a tale associated with this fort which told of the sleeping knights of King Arthur which are said to dwell within. All at once I knew the true meaning of the story! The knights had now been awakened... the knights were the Fae! Sleeping, waiting for the day when they would return once more to the surface as beings of light.

I wandered over to the very edge of the cliff and sat with my legs wrapped around a young oak tree which was perched precariously over the precipice.

I was sitting right on top of where I now knew the fairy gateway to be. I could see the car park far below my feet and the forest rolling off into the distance ahead of me. Below and to my left I could see a long slope of bare rock reaching all the way from the clifftop to the base of the hill.

Closing my eyes I could envision the days of long ago when beings of light happily danced and played and cartwheeled down the long slope, to the amazement of any local people who happened to be out wandering on these auspicious nights.

With a slight sense of vertigo I hauled myself back up and went to explore the hilltop further. I soon came across a strange shaped rock that looked invitingly like a throne.

I couldn't resist settling down into it and as soon as I did so I found myself uttering the following words:

"O fairies of the sacred hill
I come not here to wish you ill
I come here but to send you forth
To east, south, west and north
To carry forth across this land
The members of the secret band."

I then stood up from the 'chair', surprised with myself again! I wandered over to the cliff edge, this time to a deep crevice in the rock that overlooked the wooded gorge containing one of the raging rivers. A dangerous looking path seemed to lead down through the crevice to the cliff face where it turned a corner and disappeared from view.

It made me think of tales of the fairy treasure that was said to be hidden in this hill and I wondered if any of them were true and where this mysterious path led.

I closed my eyes and summoned Atheron again, but he had other things on his mind:

"It's time to step into your power!" Atheron told me. "Time to become one of the beings of light!"

It's a message that I had received several times recently, but I still did not fully understand what it meant.

"Most will be left behind in this fourth world, but some will ascend to the fifth world to join the shining ones. Others will be inspired to follow, but your real job here is to help prepare the world for this coming shift."

He was referring to the Hopi prophesy that I had learned about in Arizona. They believe that this present world, which they call the fourth world, will soon be coming to an end, and only those who remain of one heart and follow the teachings of their god Maasaw will survive to populate the coming fifth world. But Atheron seemed to be giving me a slightly different message, that somehow some people would 'ascend' from this world, leaving the old world behind. To my mind this meant that those who ascended would enter a different reality, a different consciousness, while to those who were left behind it would appear like nothing had happened. My understanding was still rather vague, but it would all become much clearer soon...

I stepped back from that hollow place near the cliff edge and decided to go searching for Ffynon Ddu, the black spring. I continued down the path that passed down the spine of the hill until eventually I came to a tiny little rivulet of water that passed over the path. "This must be it!" I thought. Now all I had to do was follow it to its source.

I scrambled through bracken and briars for a couple of hundred yards until I noticed that the gurgling rivulet to my right was no longer there. I backtracked a little and there hidden under a mass of brambles and ferns was the spring, bubbling up from between some rocks.

After dowsing to ascertain if this spring carried the correct vibration, I placed a crystal deep into its source, energised it, and then drank the water.

I could see the web of light in the sky that connected this fairy fort to all the others, immediately it brought to my mind another one of the Hopi prophesies, that one day a web would cover the entire land. This has been interpreted by some as meaning the internet, but was this the real web that was prophesied? I then saw all the springs of fresh water, and the web of energy that they wove over the land too. The male energy of the sky web, and the female energy of the earth/ water web.

I sank deeper into a trance and was told that I should soon ascend into the light and leave this mortal body behind. Its worries and concerns were not mine. My work here would soon be done, the old would die and the new would soon be reborn.

Suddenly I felt a powerful presence to my right, it was the god Pan! I felt humbled and greeted him as my master.

"I am not your master," he retorted. "Your love of the wildwoods comes from your past lives that you're still holding on to. You must fully let this go before you can ascend into the light."

I knew that he was right, but right now I did not feel ready to let go of my attachments to this earth and all its wild wonders.

I was then given a revelation concerning the shamanic worldview of lower, middle and upper worlds.

The lower world is the previous third world, where mankind and nature were one. The upper world is the coming fifth world, a magical, spiritual realm where the current laws of nature do not apply. I had nothing to fear from the fifth world, nature is still there, but in the fifth world it would assume its perfect form and I could communicate directly with nature's devas.

"Step into your power! Become Aurvandil!"

Coming back down to earth I returned to my human body and continued walking through the woods, down the slope on the far side, and down to the river encased in a golden autumnal forest. Despite the cold and gloomy weather I was thinking about how attached I was to this enchanted world with all its natural wonders. I didn't feel it was time to leave it all behind, not yet anyway.

Castell Dinas Bran, Gwyn ap Nudd

16th November

Castell Dinas Bran near Llangollen in Wales is the place where legend says St. Collen was invited to the court of the fairy king Gwyn ap Nudd. The story says that he climbed the hill and entered a magnificent hall of richly attired courtiers. There he was offered all the food, drink and entertainment his heart could desire by the fairy king who was seated upon a golden throne; but St. Collen refused to believe the illusion and he threw holy water over them all which made them disappear without a trace, leaving him alone on the hillside.

I arrived in Llangollen on a dank, cold, misty afternoon in November. It was already getting late so it did not seem like the right time to head up to the summit. I contented myself instead with wandering around the fairy-haunted woods below. Local folklore tells of an ancient walnut tree near Llandyn hall where the fairies used to hold their weddings at night.

I found a likely looking spot that fit the description, but the tree was no longer there. It was chopped down in the 19th century, but not before the fairies had their revenge, as a man was killed by a falling branch during the process!

I reached the base of the hill called Dinas Bran but the summit was barely visible through the mist, just a hint of ruined walls visible now and then. A sheep coughing sounded eerily human, the atmosphere was sombre. I could sense the presence of the fairy king up there but now was not the right time to pay him a visit, I would return the next day.

* * *

I was greeted in the morning by bright sunshine, what a relief! I set off early to Dinas Bran and parked in a lane behind the hill to save on climbing time. The valley below me was still filled with early morning mist, so I wandered down through the fairy woods to soak up the magical atmosphere.

I recalled another tale told of the area around Dinas Bran where a shepherd had an encounter with the fairy folk in a wooded glade called Nant Yr Ellyllon. He met a small man playing the most magical music on a fiddle while the fairies danced all around. Unable to resist he joined in the dance and was unable to stop until his master arrived in the morning and broke the spell.

I sat in the woods above Llandyn Hall and meditated, hoping to make some connection with the Fae there, but all I could sense was Gwyn ap Nudd up on the hilltop, waiting for me! Clearly that was where I was meant to be!

I couldn't put it off any longer so up I climbed. The walk was a lot less difficult than I thought it was going to be, so I soon found myself near the top. I came first to the shallow remains of a ditch, that probably once surrounded the ancient hillfort that crowned this hill. I felt like I should say some words before I stepped inside, so I walked around the edge of the ditch chanting over and over:

"Gwyn ap Nudd,
Lord of Annwn,
I ask your permission to enter!"

I could feel the energy building, something big was about to happen! I stepped forward:

"I am Aurvandil, the luminous wanderer. I come here bringing the light. The light of the evening star. The light from above."

I crossed the ditch and approached an archway in the ruined walls of the ancient castle.

Gwyn ap Nudd was standing there in his shining black armour and greeted me: "You are most welcome here Aurvandil!"

I walked through the archway and felt myself stepping into another world.

A large banquet hall was filled with much revelry and music. I sat at the high table beside Gwyn ap Nudd and he offered me food and wine. I felt like I was a powerful and respected Fae lord like him, my white silks contrasting with his magnificent black armour.

I stood up and my crystal-tipped wand glowed brilliantly in my hand as I held it aloft.

"I come here to bring the light and the energy you need! No longer must you live underground. It is time to return to the world above!"

The hall erupted into a loud cheer as they held their drinks aloft and celebrated.

I opened my eyes and found that I was not alone in Castell Dinas Bran. A German photographer was there, taking photos for an article about Arthurian sites in Wales. The castle is linked to the grail legends through its association with King Bran. I was hoping that he would be leaving soon, so that I could perform my ritual in peace, but he lingered, taking photos of the fort from every possible angle.

I could feel the Fae growing restless: "What is he waiting for?" they were saying.

Eventually I could wait no longer and with the photographer still hanging around the periphery I stepped into the centre of the fort and started to tune in to the energies.

I could feel the energy building like a lightning storm about to explode. I started to feel light-headed and cast a magic circle around myself. I raised my wand above my head and as I did so, the lightning struck! The energy coursed through my body directly into the hill, a huge amount of energy!

I planted my wand into the ground to anchor the energies there.

All the while the energy was still flowing down from the sky and into the ground, filling the whole hill with a matrix of white light. I could feel the Fae being transformed into beings of light, and could see them flowing out of the hillside in great, streaming, serpent-like torrents, up into the sky.

Gwyn ap Nudd stood before me, no longer dark he was now composed entirely of white light covered in streams of iridescent colours like some being from a higher dimension. He thanked me for what I had done. I could see the web of light connecting this hilltop with countless similar places of power all over the world.

The Unity Consciousness Grid! Was this it? I had just been reading about it, and how it was preparing the world for a shift in consciousness and the ascension the next level of being. Was I here in Britain doing my own small bit to contribute, like so many other lightworkers all over the world? I had just been reading about how the ancient Maya had been exiled underground, awaiting the fifth world when they could return to earth as beings of light. Were the Fae our version of the ancient Maya? Weren't they also forced underground long ago, and were they not now returning?

Suddenly everything that I had been doing was starting to make sense. Anchoring energies. The grid. The return of the Fae. Raising the consciousness of the people by energising the water. The ascension. Those that will rise to the next level and those who will be left behind. A new world created. Nature in harmony, vibrant and alive. The Lord of the Wild claiming back his domain. The Fae who will once more walk over the face of the earth, and the enlightened ones who will create a new world!

Looking around the castle I noticed a little enclosure that looked like a shrine, it was facing due west. I left an offering there and give thanks.

I walked down the hillside and watched two jays chasing each other through the trees. The magical wooded glade ahead was surely Nant yr Ellyllon, the one mentioned in the folk tales! The name meant 'Glade of the Shining Ones' where, if you are not careful, you could spend all night dancing with the fairies!

North Wales, Holy Wells and a Holy Mountain

18th November

After my experience with Gwyn ap Nudd on Dinas Bran I then travelled across North Wales investigating several of the holy wells there and energising them with my crystals.

St. Tecla's Well (where epilepsy could be cured by carrying a chicken under your arm!) was in an idyllic location by the river on the edge of a small village. It seemed to be well looked after.

St. Dyfnog's Well was in a magical wooded gully behind a church and had a large bathing pool where I was guided to go in and take an icy dip! I amplified the healing properties of the water there using my wand.

St. Trillo's well was in a tiny chapel on the seashore, inside the smallest church in Wales! Legend says that St. Trillo was drawn to the well by a column of light issuing forth from the ground. I ended up sitting through a Eucharist service there in the tiny church in order to sample the well's waters!

St. Tudno's Well, on the Great Orm's Head, was overgrown and forgotten, and clogged with plastic rubbish which I spent some time removing.

* * *

Next on my list was St. Seriol's Well at Penmon Priory on the island of Anglesey. I was quite excited to be going to the sacred druidic island of Anglesey, and my first view over the Menai Strait was directly towards the remote corner of the island where Penmon Priory lay.

After crossing the Menai bridge I arrived at Penmon Priory quite late in the day. I had a quick look at the ancient and impressive dovecote and then went directly over to the holy well, which lay just behind the priory. The short winter day was already drawing to a close, but a local family were still there, and the children were gazing at the coins deposited in the crystal-clear waters of the well. So I took the opportunity to explore the area around the well and look back towards the priory. I had a stunning view of the ancient priory sitting by the water in the clear evening light.

When I returned the family had gone, so I finally had the place to myself. I sat on the stone seat inside the wellhouse and meditated. I didn't get any messages in there but was drawn instead to the circular foundations outside, the remains of the ancient hermit's cell of St. Seriol.

The cell seemed to be filled with a yellow, glowing light, inside which flickered golden tendrils.

I cautiously stepped into the energy of the cell and stood directly in its centre, where I planted my wand purposefully into the ground.

Golden energy then seemed to fan out from my wand in all directions, like the spokes of a great wheel, connecting it to the walls of the cell. A beam of white light then shot out skywards from the tip of my wand, seemingly all the way up to the stars. My wand now seemed to be connected to a distant star hidden deep in the heavens, and it felt like some kind of communication was going on, like my wand was receiving a download of some sort.

The communication finished, but I didn't quite know what it meant, it felt like whatever information my wand was now carrying was there for me to use somehow. So I decided to get out my dowsing rods to try to find out what had just happened.

I summoned the white light down from the sky into my rods, and put up my protections, but instead of the light entering into the crown of my head as it usually does, it landed in front of me and instantly transformed into the glowing white figure of Merlin!

Merlin spoke to me. He told me I had performed my tasks well. I had not abused my power, and was ready to ascend to the next level, when I would become Merlin too! What did he mean by this? He told me to go to the highest point on Ynys Mon and meet him there.

I walked back to my car in the gloomy twilight and said hello to the local cat, who seemed to be waiting for me and was meowing loudly. I sat in the car and got out my map. The weather was cold and damp, and I could feel a sniffle coming on. I did not relish the prospect of having to climb a mountain! Luckily for me though Anglesey (Ynys Mon) does not have any mountains as such, just some moderately high hills!

A quick search on the internet soon directed me to Holyhead Mountain, the highest point on Anglesey. Although not strictly on Anglesey, as Holy Island is separated from Ynys Mon by a narrow strait, I instinctively knew that it was the right place. The Holy Island! Where else? Its holy name is not Christian but goes back to ancient pagan times when the druids ruled Anglesey. It was the holiest place in Wales, and Holy Island was at that time the most sacred place in Anglesey. Truly a place of power!

So I started my car engine, drove over to Holyhead in the dark, and then awaited the dawn.

* * *

It was a chilly, windy, damp day in late November. My throat was getting sore, my nose was running and my limbs ached, so I drove as near as I could to Holyhead Mountain, up a farm track near its south face. The mountain looked daunting, with sheer rock faces, but my map indicated a path of some sort to the top, so off I trotted, feeling better with each step as I took in the clean fresh air.

I soon reached the top and walked over to a craggy point on the east side of the summit and stood facing into a strong wind. I held my wand in front of me and meditated while the wind buffeted me.

Soon I could hear myself chanting, a deep guttural tone sung directly into the wind, which seemed to carry right through me and deep into the mountain.

"The old ones will awaken!" I thought as I heard the sound reverberating through hidden underground caverns.

Suddenly Merlin appeared before me, a giant, huge and powerful, composed entirely of white light. I too then grew in size and stood there as Aurvandil, tall and powerful, another giant glowing being of light. We stood there facing each other on the mountaintop, as equals. Merlin praised me again, and told me that I had now completed my quest of initiation. He told me I could now ascend to the next level. He touched the blue teardrop crystal that sat on my forehead and it glowed. Was this my third eye opening? Had I now come full circle? From my initiation in Merlin's Cave to my ascension on Holyhead Mountain?

The blue gem on my forehead glowed brightly, as did the white crystal on my wand. They both glowed brilliantly with a blinding light. I raised my wand into the air and called down a huge and powerful column of white light from the sky which filled the whole mountain with its energy. So powerful was the energy that soon the whole island seemed to be filled with it. I connected this place of power into the grid of light that covered the whole land, but somehow this felt different, not just another node of energy but an entire hub, huge and powerful! The holy island of the druids, the power centre of Anglesey, the power centre of Wales, the Holy Isle of Merlin! I could feel my body trembling as the huge column of energy coursed through me, down into the mountain and then outwards into the web that covered the whole earth.

As the energy slowly subsided I could feel myself returning to my own body again, back to the windswept mountain top and the wild nature of the island of Britain. My body had been physically shaking but now I felt calm. Merlin told me that my task for the present time was now done. I should now just relax and await further developments.

I started to set off walking back down the mountain but soon came to a pool that I hadn't noticed on my way up. I felt compelled to place a crystal in the pool and also some of the water that I had collected from St. Trillo's Well. This mountain would now become a magical place I thought, full of dancing lights and strange phenomena. Local people would notice the difference, the old magic would return.

As I reached the bottom of the hill I looked back up at the summit. In my mind's eye I could still see the giant forms of Merlin and Aurvandil standing up there.

"Once giants walked the earth," I thought.

And maybe soon they will again...

Epilogue

Merlin's quest was now complete, but the adventure was only just beginning...

There were so many questions that still remained unanswered. Who was the faery woman who awaited me in the Otherworld? Why did Neptune ask me to fetch him his undines? What was this crystal grid I was helping to create? And what was my true purpose for being incarnated here on earth at this time?

These questions and others I hope to answer in subsequent books in this series, including many more adventures to sacred sites and magical places all over Britain, Ireland and the rest of the world!

About the Author

Rob Wildwood

Rob Wildwood was born in a seaside town in Yorkshire and spent his childhood exploring the local countryside and the myths and folklore of the North York Moors. He was introduced to Norse shamanism in his early twenties and had a keen interest in history, particularly the history of Britain's pagan past. He spent many years taking part in Viking festivals all over Europe and spent some years living in Scandinavia where he expanded his online business called *The Jelling Dragon* which sells hand-crafted reproductions of Viking artefacts.

He was fascinated by the animist beliefs of primitive cultures, which see everything in nature as being imbued with spirit. This led Rob to travel the world experiencing indigenous cultures, including spending time with the Kalahari Bushmen, the nomadic Penan of Borneo and the forest Naikas of India.

These travels revived his interest in shamanism and he eventually returned to England to study core shamanism in Glastonbury. While there he also became involved in the faery scene where people dressed as magical beings and even practiced a form of pagan faery spirituality. This marked the beginning of another long adventure where he sought out and photographed magical places all over Britain, tuning in to the energies of these places and receiving channelled messages using shamanic journeying techniques. This led directly to the publication of his first book *Magical Places of Britain* which is a richly illustrated photographic guide to the folklore of these sites. His spiritual adventures and visionary experiences while visiting these sites have now finally been collated into this book you are holding called *The Land of the Fae.*

Rob has subsequently visited many more sacred sites and magical places, both in Britain and while travelling extensively around the world, including sites in Ireland, Scandinavia, North America, Hawaii, New Zealand, Indonesia, India and eventually Australia, where he spent several seasons studying Aboriginal culture and exploring the dreamtime legends of the sacred landscape there.

These experiences led to the publication of his book *Primal Awareness* which seeks to answer the question: "Why did mankind become so separated from nature and world of spirit?" The book also offers exercises that seek to redress this imbalance within each of us.

Rob also became interested in dowsing, ley lines and earth energies, and has followed ley lines extensively across Britain and Europe. He eventually settled down in Glastonbury, Somerset where he still lives and is self-employed as an author, photographer and tour guide. For more information visit his website and Facebook page:

www.themagicalplaces.com
www.facebook.com/themagicalplaces

Magical Places of Britain (2013) - Wyldwood Publishing

The companion guide to Land of the Fae! A beautifully illustrated photographic guide to some of Britain's most magical places covering many of the places mentioned in the Land of the Fae, from enchanted forests, haunted waters, mystic mountains and sacred springs to fairy hills, magic caves and other places of mystery and enchantment in the British landscape.

Primal Awareness (2018) - Moon Books

A short history of mankind's separation from nature and what we can do to reconnect.

Focusing on the origins of Western culture and belief systems, from ancient agriculture to modern industry, from primitive religion to monotheism, Primal Awareness explains how we became separated from nature and how, throughout history, these belief systems and social models have imposed a life of servitude and hardship upon millions of people. It also illustrates how modern technology and the modern scientific world view are currently causing the destruction of our natural environment. How can we overcome this separation, and reconnect with nature and spirit once again?

Afterword by Alphedia Arara

I hope you enjoyed this journey into the land of the magical unseen realms. I was clearly guided to meet Rob Wildwood in 2010 when the Fairies told me that I should attend a workshop at the Three Wishes Faery Festival in Cornwall, an event which I was already attending as a speaker. It has been a privilege to have had many Fae adventures with Rob over the years since his first initiation by Merlin in Tintagel. If you follow your intuition and inner guidance you too can have your own Fae adventures by allowing yourself to be transported into the magic and wonder of the enchanted realms!

Alphedia Arara is the founder of Elemental Beings, which is based in Scotland. She teaches people how to communicate with nature spirits, and is the author of *Messages from Nature's Guardians*. She is also is an international spiritual facilitator, channelling many different beings of light. She runs regular workshops and earth healing retreats, with a distance option to allow people from all around the world to join in with her work. For more information visit www.elementalbeings.co.uk or find her on Facebook and Instagram.

APPENDIX

Arizona, Sacred Landscape of the Hopi

October

I had become intrigued by stories concerning an ancient carved stone in the deserts of Arizona known as the Hopi Prophecy Stone. The Hopi people had guarded this stone for centuries and kept it away from prying eyes, but now I felt compelled to take a journey away from my homeland to discover its secrets.

I started by exploring the sacred landscape around Sedona, an area famous for its spiritual energy and natural vortex sites. I explored many sacred sites and ancient Anasazi ruins around there, but it was in the Land of the Hopi, far off in the high desert to the North, that my real quest would begin.

The Hopi people are Native Americas who have lived in Arizona for at least 800 years. Unlike the plains Indians further North they live in stone dwellings and so are known as pueblo Indians. They live in an isolated part of the country, on three mesas (high plateaus flanked by cliffs). Until recently they lived a simple spiritual life of growing corn and performing seasonal ceremonies. They believe that they were given this sacred land in order to preserve their culture and ancient way of life. The land is dry, and life-giving rains will only come if the spirits (kachinas) are kept happy, so the regular observance of rituals and a deep humility and reverence towards nature are central to their culture.

The Hopi are secretive, and they are wary of outsiders, so it was not simply a matter of marching in there and asking to see their prophecy stone, I had to tread delicately and make contact first.

I started by taking a tour from Sedona with a lady called Sandra who had an intimate connection with the Hopi. We were allowed unprecedented access to some of the traditional stone dwellings. People still lived in these traditional houses and outside we saw Hopi women delivering baskets for the coming basket ceremony and carrying bags of corn for a wedding. We were also introduced to the idea of kachinas, spirits that come in hundreds of different guises representing the various forces of nature. The Hopi make an art of creating brightly-painted little wooden statues of these kachinas. We visited a fascinating store where local Hopi people would bring traditional handcrafts to sell, including many handmade kachinas. At the end of our tour I planned to return to the store later to discover more.

Back in Sedona I had many more adventures visiting vortex sites and energising the landscape with crystals. At Palatki ruins I found an ancient sun wheel painted onto the rock face and decided to meditate there. When I opened my eyes I noticed some brightly coloured feathers on the ground nearby that seemed to have been sheared off, either by a knife or by a bird of prey. I felt like there was something special about these orange-tipped feathers and so I decided to take them with me.

A psychic woman called Kathleen gave me a reading while I was in Sedona and told me I was "a very powerful being from another world," and that I had "come here on an important quest, carrying and anchoring energies." How did she know?! She also told me that I was afraid of stepping into my power, which was probably true, although I didn't quite know what she meant.

I felt very tired and spaced out that evening; I felt like I'd had enough of the weird energies of Sedona, I had a mission to do, so in the morning I woke up early and raring to go! This time I would be travelling to the Hopi lands alone in a rental car. I did not know anyone there and did not even know if I would be welcomed by the Hopi, but I thought that the craft shop might be a good place to start.

The shop owner Joseph was of European descent but had married a local Hopi woman and had now been fully initiated into one of the clans. He told me to talk to a local glass blower by the name of Ramson, so I travelled over to his glass-blowing workshop and found him to be very friendly and accommodating. He told me all kinds of stories about Hopi culture and mythology, but when my questions got a little too deep he said: "If I tell you that I'll have to kill you!"

I discovered that the Hopi have many different clans, and that each clan has its own secret ceremonies. Many of these ceremonies are carried out in bell-shaped underground chambers known as kivas. Only the initiated are allowed to go anywhere near these kivas.

I returned to the craft shop and then noticed a car outside that had feathers hanging from the rear view mirror. They were exactly the same as the feathers that I had picked up at Palatki! Joseph told me that the feathers were from a bird called the orange-shafted flicker which was sacred to the Hopi and was carried by them for good luck in travel. Only the Hopi were allowed to take them, it was illegal for a non-native to be carrying them!

Joseph told me that it was completely forbidden to visit any of the sacred sites myself, the only possible way was with a Hopi guide, but none were currently available. So what was I to do? Despondently I returned to Ramson's workshop to see if he could give me any pointers, hopefully he would not say he had to kill me this time!

When I arrived there I got a surprise, a Hopi guy called Bertram was there with a tour group! I got talking to him and told him I would like to go to Taawa Canyon to see the petroglyphs (rock carvings) and amazingly he told me that was exactly where they were going next and I could tag along if I liked. What a stroke of luck! It seemed like I was always being guided to be in the right place at the right time!

Taawa Canyon was completely covered in ancient petroglyphs: stars, spirals, concentric circles, sun wheels, snakes, people carrying corn, gods, spirits and strange amphibian beings. The ground was littered with pottery shards from the ancient Anasazi people, ancestors of the Hopi, and in one corner there was an ancient 'birthing chamber.'

Bertram explained the meaning of many of the petroglyphs but particularly intriguing was a symbol of four concentric circles which represented emergence into the fourth world. The Hopi believe that we are currently in the fourth incarnation of this world, and that they emerged into this fourth world from the previous third world at a very sacred location at the bottom of the grand canyon known as the Sipapu. The Sipapu itself is represented in the petroglyphs as a point within a circle, and I discovered that the Sipapu actually still exists. It is a natural salt dome where salt water bubbles from the ground leaving deposits that eventually form a huge dome. It takes a couple of days of very hot, dusty hiking to reach the dome which lies at the bottom of the world's biggest canyon, and it is so sacred that only the initiated are allowed to go anywhere near it.

Before we left Taawa Canyon I asked Bertram the burning question: could he take me to see the Prophecy Stone? He was a little hesitant at first but eventually he agreed to meet me again in four days time to take me there. I was elated! My quest may finally reach its conclusion!

I filled the intervening days by first visiting the Wupatki Blowhole, a sacred site where a constant stream of air blows out of the earth from deep underground caverns. I took a shamanic journey there into the underworld:

I was an elven knight riding on a horse and wearing a shining skull-cap helmet. I was looking out over a magical land.

I got the feeling that this underworld (or lower world) was the previous third world as described by the Hopi. A lost age of the earth that was left behind when we emerged into this fourth world.

Breathing in the air from this underworld blowhole made me feel quite spaced out, giving everything an Otherworldly and magical appearance.

After exploring more Anasazi ruins, which seemed to litter the landscape around there, I decided to take a journey to the Grand Canyon. I visited some of the more well-known lookouts on the south rim before heading to the Back country Office to get information on the Hopi Salt Trail, something that I planned to go and explore later...

The next day I returned to Hopi land and met up with Bertram at Old Oraibi. He didn't waste any time and drove me directly to the Hopi Prophecy Stone. I was a bit disappointed at how easy it was to get there, I didn't feel like the mythical goal of my quest should be so easily achieved! But I did hear rumours that this perhaps was only a copy and that the original prophecy stone was hidden in the mountains somewhere and has never been seen by outsiders.

The Prophecy Stone stands about four metres high and on it is a very unusual carving. There are two parallel lines, the top one ends in a zig-zig which indicates destruction, while the bottom one shows people planting corn, which maintains natural harmony. It is a warning that if mankind continues on its current course then it will mean destruction for us all. Beneath this stands their creator god Maasaw. He holds a 'gourd of ashes' which will be dropped on our world in a great cataclysm. The Hopi believe that if they can maintain their simple spiritual existence, living close to nature and growing corn, that they will be safe on their mesas and will avoid the coming destruction.

So this is what I had come here to learn. That mankind must raise its consciousness and forego materiality in order to avoid destruction. Perhaps the work I was doing was my own small contribution towards this?

After the coming destruction the survivors, those who remained true to their spiritual path, will emerge into the new world, the coming fifth world.

* * *

I did eventually find the Hopi salt trail, in a remote part of the Grand Canyon, far from civilisation.

This was the place where young Hopi men would undertake a grueling initiation, walking over 90 miles through the desert and down into the Grand Canyon to collect salt. The trail eventually leads to the sacred Sipapu, the place of emergence of the Hopi people, but I only ventured a short way down the very steep and rocky trail.

While there I discovered more ancient petroglyphs and two huge pinnacles of rock known as the War Twins which seemed to guard the descent. Under one of the war twins I found ancient pahos (prayer sticks) which had been deposited there. I had no intention of taking them but I wanted to have a closer look so put my hand into the crevice to touch the sticks. As I did so a large chunk of rock fell off right next to me but luckily I was able jump out of the way before being injured. It seemed like the spirits still guarded this place! I felt like I had seen and learned enough. My adventures in the Hopi lands were now over. It was time to go home.

THE HORNED GOD
LADY OF NATURE
PAN
GAIA
FAERY KING & QUEEN
NEPTUNE
LORD OF THE OCEAN
MINOR FAE
WOOD ELVES
FAERIES / ELF LORDS
OCEAN FAE
MERMAIDS
LIGHT ELVES
& DARK ELVES
HOBS
BOGGLES
SELKIES
REDCAPS

The Otherworld of the Fae
ELEMENTALS
PLANT SPIRITS
ANIMAL SPIRITS
WOLVES
TREE SPIRITS
AIR SYLPHE
FIRE DRAGON
DEER
WATER
EARTH
FROGS
WATER NYMPH
WORMS
BIRCH PEOPLE
BIRDS
WATER HAG
GNOMES
INSECTS
WATER SPRITES

GLOSSARY

Avatar – A projection of oneself that is sent out into the *spirit world.*
Birch people – *Tree spirits* associated with birch trees.
Boggles – Small *fae* with pointy ears that live underground in colonies.
Celtic Church – An early form of Christianity practiced in Ireland and the British Isles, possibly incorporating elements of Druidry.
Dark Elves – Dark *faeries* that usually have little to do with humans.
Dragons - Powerful *elementals* associated with earth energies and fire.
Druidry – The *pagan* religion of the *druids.*
Druids – Priests of the ancient Celtic *pagan* religion.
Dwarves – Dark *fae* who dwell underground.
Elementals – *Nature spirits* that are associated with one of the four natural elements of Earth, Air, Fire and Water.
Elfland – The *Otherworld* of the *Fae.*
Elflords – Noble *faeries,* also known as *light elves.*
Elfin-spirits (Elves) – Mindlessly playful *fae* often given to trickery or mischief, they have olive green or brown frog-like skin, and are lithe and skinny, slightly shorter than humans. Note: the word Elf can also be used to refer to *faeries.*
Fae – Various races of beings from the *Otherworld.* They are all humanoid in form, but of varying size, from tiny *hobs* and *boggles* to the tall and elegant *faeries.* Note: They do not generally have wings.
Faeries – Tall, beautiful fae from the *Otherworld,* also known as the *Sidhe,* or trooping *fairies.* They are generally human-sized or taller, and they do not have wings.
Faery King – A king of the *faeries.*
Faery Queen – A queen of the *faeries.*
Fairies – 1. Traditional name for the *faeries.*
2. The *fae* in general.
3. Small winged air *elementals* (sylphs).
Fairyland – The *Otherworld.*
Gaia – The all-powerful *spirit* of the Earth.
Gnomes – Small earth *elementals.*
Gods & Goddesses – Very powerful *spirits* that rule over a major aspect of nature. e.g. *Neptune* for the sea.

Green man – The vegetation *god*, responsible for the growth of all plants.
Gwyn ap Nudd – *Faery king* from Welsh mythology.
Hecate – Greek *goddess* of dark magic, often associated with crossroads.
Hob – Small household *fae* from the north of England.
Hobgoblin – A powerful *hob*.
Hobman – a *hob*.
Horned God – The male nature *god*. He has stag's antlers on his head, and is the lord of all animals. See also *Pan*.
Imp – Small malevolent *fae*.
Jenny Greenteeth – A malevolent water *spirit* in the form of an old hag with sharp teeth and pondweed in her hair.
Light elves – Light *faeries* who are noble in both manner and bearing.
Merlin – Celtic wizard, head *druid* and *spirit guide*.
Mermaids – Female water *fae* with fish tails who live in the sea.
Nature Spirits – *Spirits* that are associated with a plant, animal or natural phenomena.
Neptune – Roman *god* of the sea.
Otherworld – The hidden world that underlies our mundane world, visible only to those with second sight. It is home to the *Fae* and to all the *nature spirits*. The laws of physics, as we understand them, do not apply there.
Pagan – One who practices the ancient pre-Christian religion which was closely associated with nature.
Pan – Greek *god* with goat's horns and cloven hooves, he is the lord of all nature.
Queen Mab – British *Fairy Queen*, equivalent to the Irish Faery *Queen Maeve*.
Queen Maeve - Irish *Fairy Queen* and *spirit guide*.
Rath – A *faery* fort, a place where *faeries* live.
Redcap – Tiny humanoid *fae* wearing traditional clothes and red caps.
Selkies – Female *fae* with seal skins who live in the sea.
Shining Ones – Shining beings in humanoid form who descend from the skies. Their origin is unknown, they could be *fae*, angels or extra-terrestrials.
Sidhe – The Irish Gaelic name for the *faeries*. In Scots Gaelic it is spelt Sith, but both are pronounced "Shee."

Spirit – The spiritual essence of something. Its *Otherworld* counterpart.
Spirit guide – Personal spiritual helper and advisor from the *Otherworld.*
Spirit of the Land – A powerful *spirit* that embodies the spiritual essence of a whole landscape.
Spirit World – The *Otherworld.*
Sprites – Tiny water *elementals.*
Tree spirit – The *spirit* of a tree.
Troll – Earth *spirit* from Scandinavia.
Underworld – An alternative name for the *Otherworld*, particularly its lower dimensions.
Undine – See *mermaid.*
Water Hag – See *Jenny Greenteeth.*
Water Nymphs – Female nature *spirits* associated with freshwater springs.
Wood Elves – See *Elfin Spirits.*

GLOSSARY OF LANDSCAPE FEATURES

Allt – a stream (Scots-Gaelic)
Beck - a stream (Yorkshire)
Burn – a stream (Scottish)
Carr – a marsh with trees (Yorkshire)
Castell – castle (Welsh)
Coille – a woodland (Scots-Gaelic)
Combe – a short valley (SW England)
Craig – rock (Scottish-Gaelic)
Dale – a valley (Yorkshire)
Dinas – fort (Welsh)
Eilean – island (Scots-Gaelic)
Fairy mound – a small rounded hill or burial mound
Gill – an indentation in the hillside created by a small stream (Yorkshire)
Glen – a valley (Scottish)
Gorge – a canyon or ravine, usually with a stream running though it
Gully – a ravine created by flowing water
Head – the high end of a valley where the streams emerge
Howe – a burial mound (Yorkshire)
Knoll – a small hill or mound
Loch – lake (Scottish)
Moor – treeless uplands clad in heather
Motte – a mound on which the keep of a (usually wooden) castle once stood
Nant – a glade (Welsh)
Rath – a circular enclosure or ring fort (Irish)
Rigg – a ridge of hills (Yorkshire)
Scar – a cliff (Yorkshire)
Sithean - fairy knoll (Scots-Gaelic)
Tigh - a house (Scots-Gaelic)
Tom – a knoll (Scots-Gaelic)
Ynys – an island (Welsh)